The Tax Dilemma:
PRAYING for
PAYING for PEACE WAR

This volume is part of the Christian Peace Shelf Series. Inquiries about the Christian Peace Shelf are invited.

The Tax Dilemma:
PRAYING FOR PEACE, PAYING FOR WAR

Donald D. Kaufman

Introduction by John K. Stoner

Focal Pamphlet 30

HERALD PRESS
Scottdale, Pennsylvania
Kitchener, Ontario

Library of Congress Cataloging in Publication Data

Kaufman, Donald D
  The tax dilemma.

  (Focal pamphlet; 30)
  Includes bibliographical references.
    1. Taxation—United States. 2. Tax evasion—United
States. 3. Disarmament—Economic aspects—United States.
I. Title.
HJ2381.K32   336.2'00973   78-11279
ISBN 0-8361-1872-3

THE TAX DILEMMA: Praying for Peace, Paying for War
Copyright ©1978 by Herald Press, Scottdale, Pa. 15683
  Published simultaneously in Canada by Herald Press,
    Kitchener, Ont. N2G 4M5
Library of Congress Catalog Card Number: 78-11279
International Standard Book Number: 0-8361-1872-3
Design: Alice B. Shetler

10 9 8 7 6 5 4 3 2

CONTENTS

AUTHOR'S PREFACE

Until the middle of the twentieth century it was an appropriate and valid Christian witness to refuse bodily participation in war. But many have come to believe that the refusal of military service alone is no longer an adequate response to the military demons which threaten to destroy the people on Planet Earth. The nuclear age, coupled with the strategy of deterence, has made it possible for nations to play an extremely dangerous game of competitive survival. The arms race and military spending have escalated to unbelievable levels. The astronomical amounts of money being spent for "national defense" and the consequent theft from the poor of this world suggest that war taxes are too monumental an issue to be ignored. What if Jeanette Rankin, the first woman to serve in the United States Congress, is right? "All they that live by the sword shall perish by taxes."[1]

For twenty years or more there has been a renewed awareness of the ethical implications of paying Federal taxes. Yet, because the church is conservative in implementing its faith and because our preconditioning resists change no consensus on the issue has yet emerged. Through our voluntary or involuntary participation in war as taxpayers, we are party to injustice that staggers the mind.

Most persons who attempt to interpret the past also seek to understand the present and something of the future. Reflecting upon experiences of the past is often useful and certainly enlightening. If we are to have a usable past on the issue of taxes exploited for war purposes it seems necessary to gather these historical encounters into a readily accessible collection. *What Belongs to Caesar?* (Herald Press, 1969) was my first attempt to compile such information. More happenings have come to light in the years since its publication. These too may have instructive value to us who are looking for signs of God's guidance in our own time. Although the lessons of history are not easily learned, the likelihood of repeating the errors of the past is increased if we refuse to learn from our own and others' experiences. This booklet of true life happenings is offered to meet that need.

Senator George McGovern, making no pretensions about holding a pacifist position, once reminded members of the United States Senate that the administration will do well to heed the admonition of Edmund Burke, a distinguished legislator of an earlier day: "A conscientious man would be cautious how he dealt in blood." I firmly believe that war tax history has a special significance in understanding God's agenda in human history. Perhaps it is good to be challenged once again by the example of those who have tried faithfully to apply the gospel of Christ to complex and questionable tax requirements. According to Sören Kierkegaard, "The past which cannot become present is not worth remembering."

Finally, I owe a special word of appreciation to Jill Preheim Graber, James Klassen, Marilyn Klaus, Susan Wedel Krehbiel, Robert Kreider, Harold Regier, Paul M. Schrock, Perry Yoder, the members of my Koinonia group, and numerous other persons for their help in getting this book into print.

Another recruit in the Lamb's War,

Donald D. Kaufman

INTRODUCTION

"But what can I do? I am only one person." —Author Unknown

The most common response of people to the unprecedented moral crisis of the world arms race is a sense of futility. Many people will agree that the survival of the human race itself is in jeopardy. Few will agree as to what can be done about it. An even smaller number believe that they personally can do anything.

Moreover, it is distressing to observe how many people attempt to absolve themselves of any personal responsibility for the situation we are in. They blame the government, big business, fate, God, or the devil. There is a great deal of passing the buck.

Especially, of passing the buck to Caesar. In the form of taxes, that is. War taxes. Yes, the word is out: there is such a thing as taxes for war. The government, if it calls it anything, calls it defense spending. People with a commitment to speak the truth, such as Christians, have a responsibility to expose the deceptive euphemisms and call a war tax a war tax.

At which point we return to the words of our unknown author, and supply her with another quote: I can do something about the taxes I pay for war.

This book is about doing that something. Appendix D is itself worth the price of the book for the unusual brain waves which it creates. But there is much more.

The book issues a challenge to a wide audience— Christian and non-Christian. God's claim on humankind is universal. But I find the author probing the Christian conscience most directly. What does it mean for the church to be praying for peace and paying for war? Donald Kaufman explores this contradiction from many angles and draws on many sources, but all with a view to finding the path of Christian obedience.

I have heard many Christians say that they do not engage in war tax resistance or protest because it is ineffective. The government ultimately gets the money, the resister makes no impact, and the exercise is futile. Apart from the fact that this appeal for success is strange talk for people whose hero and leader ended up being crucified, I hear in this an unspoken message that also doesn't quite fit. The general demeanor of these folks toward society and government is one of studious conformity to accepted practice and one does not have to be richly endowed with imagination to infer that tax resistance or protest looks very risky to them. Which adds up to suggesting that their real reason for not engaging in tax resistance is that they think it would be too effective—in challenging accepted myths, clarifying the moral issue, and inviting the neighbor to take a similar stand.

In this regard, it might just be that the church should embrace tax resistance as the moral equivalent of disarmament. It has become fairly acceptable in at least some church circles to call on government to take risks for peace in the way of disarmament. In those circles it has not been unusual to look with some disdain on those who called for tax resistance as a form of response to the arms race. Given the meager successes of all the disarmament talks of history, including the 1978 United Nations Special Session on Disarmament, from a purely strategic point of view it might begin to occur to us that disarmament is such an intractable problem that we shall have to appeal to the people over the heads of the politicians to do something about it. But on a level deeper than calculating strategies for success, the church should be asking its members what is the *right* thing for them to do regardless of the consequences. If the generals, presidents, and ambassadors have decided to continue the arms race, shall the Christians continue to pay for it?

For the church (indeed, for any sizeable denomination of the church) to embrace war tax resistance as a spiritual commitment and a stated policy would be the moral equivalent of a government seriously embracing a policy of disarmament. Both would involve risk, both would be unprecedented, and both would be right.

But what government is ready to do the right thing on disarmament? And what church is ready to do the right on war taxes?

There are costs and risks involved.

John K. Stoner, Executive Secretary
Mennonite Central Committee Peace Section (US)
July 4, 1978

Kings

The kings of the earth are men of might,
And cities are burned for their delight,
And the skies rain death in the silent night,
    And the hills belch death all day!

But the King of Heaven, who made them all,
Is fair and gentle, and very small;
He lies in the straw, by the oxen's stall—
    Let them think of Him today!

—Joyce Kilmer

The Tax Dilemma:

PRAYING for PAYING for PEACE WAR

No Dissenting Voice

There was a time when William James could say that "war taxes are the only ones men never hesitate to pay."[2] But no longer. Just as A. J. Muste once argued "that it is not really possible to separate conscription and war"[3] today it can be said that it is no longer possible to separate tax payments from war. Taxes and war are inextricably linked together. When governments wage wars, they eventually levy taxes on the citizens to pay for them. And Will Durant reports that "in the last 3,421 years of recorded history, only 268 have seen no war."[4] Furthermore, taxes which escalate to high levels during a time of war are seldom if ever reduced to the earlier level. As a result we are faced with permanent war and the perpetual danger of escalating military budgets. Higher appropriations than ever seem likely for the 1980s.

Death and Taxes Join Hands

Governments invariably claim the right to levy taxes. Benjamin Franklin understood this fact of life when he said: "Nothing is certain but death and taxes."[5] (More recently a *Punch* cartoon noted that "what the taxpayer resents is that they don't come in that order"! Another observed that "the difference between death and taxes is that death does not get worse every time congress meets.") Despite our claims of having freedom, most citizens of the United States live in bondage to death— the death created by war tax payments. Martin Luther King, Jr., observed that his own government was "the greatest purveyor of violence in the world today." That observation is substantiated by the fact that four to seven dollars of every ten collected in taxes in the United States go to pay for wars—past, present, and projected.

15

Drafted Dollars Come First

Preoccupied as some citizens are with paying too much tax, I suggest that the crucial issue has to do with the purpose for which tax monies are used, not the amount. Presently a large portion of the federal budget is going to the Pentagon. More and more money is budgeted annually for its support. While a young person can be exempted from personally serving in the armed forces, no one is easily exempted from making contributions to the military leviathan.

There are those who for centuries have carried out the mandate of Jesus not to kill fellow human beings, but to love them, even at the risk of being killed themselves. Their commitment to love and peace, however, has not always kept them from paying taxes for military purposes. Is there not a glaring contradiction here unless people are peacemakers in *both* body and property? Why should the Christian refuse service in the army if he does not refuse to pay taxes? Is there a valid moral distinction between performing military service and paying the taxes which make war possible?

> In the days when the state asked primarily for men to go to war, we were conscientious objectors. But now the primary tool of war is money. Can we still be conscientious objectors now?[6]

Each of us is called upon to answer that crucial question.

The Bible Says—Or Does It?

For most people it is out of the question even to think of tax refusal alternatives until they are convinced that the Scriptures either allow or support such action. Many

Christians feel that there is an indisputable biblical mandate to pay all taxes just as one pays for other financial obligations. Actually it may be more nearly correct to say that the New Testament teaches neither the payment nor the refusal of all taxes. Because of this it is most urgent that we reexamine our assumptions about what the Bible says on this subject.

If we recognize the limitations of being selective, it will be helpful to examine those references which are often used to justify unquestioning obedience to governmental demands (i.e., Mark 12:13-17 and parallel passages; Matthew 17:24-27; Romans 13:1-7; and 1 Peter 2:13-17). We dare not assume that a few verses can give us the total biblical understanding or the definitive Christian point of view on church/state relations. 1 Samuel 8:10-20, Jeremiah 43:10a, Daniel chapters 3—7, Acts 5:29, Ephesians 6:12, and Revelation 13 and 19, where the institution of government is viewed more critically, are not to be overlooked.

Unless we study each passage in the context of the historical situation and in the light of the total gospel, we will hardly understand the Bible properly in such matters. One of the biggest hurdles for Christians to overcome in considering the war tax issue is the widespread assumption that the Bible speaks with one voice regarding the necessity of tax payment to the governments. People try too hard to give an evenhanded recognition to the church and the state in our society.

One of the verses in the New Testament which has provided sanction for a myriad of wrongs is Jesus' reply to the Pharisees and Herodians concerning the tax paid to Caesar. "Render to Caesar the things that are Caesar's, and to God the things that are God's" (Mark

12:17). Many believe this directive legitimizes whatever government requires of us even though we should also protest its evil course on any issue.[7] However, the text may not be interpreted in such a way as to equalize God's and Caesar's rights. The total context suggests that Jesus was making a statement in which the second clause had considerable priority over the first. For Jesus the overarching loyalty was to God and it was this loyalty which determined the character of His loyalty to Caesar. Conflicting situations were resolved for Him by His primary relationship to God.

The "half-shekel tax" referred to in Matthew 17 is definitely the temple tax which each Jew over twenty paid for the operation of the sanctuary since the time of the Exodus. Although Jesus opposed the compulsory nature of the tax He definitely chose to support the Jewish pattern of worship. Following the destruction of the temple in AD 70, this tax was appropriated by Roman officials for Jupiter Capitolinus. We do know that Christians refused to pay taxes for Caesar's pagan temple in Rome. For this reason, we can understand how erroneous it is to deduce from this story about the temple tax a command for the payment of all taxes.[8]

Paul's letter to Roman Christians is carefully organized. The development of his letter suggests that chapters 12 and 13 bear a close relationship to each other and definitely belong together. Is it not significant that the author prefaces his discussion of "authorities" (13:1-7) with a long discussion on the practical implications of Christian love (12:1-21)? Several scholars are convinced that the writer expects Christians to discriminate between the demands of Caesar and the demands of God, giving to each only his due, "refusing to give to

Caesar what belongs to God."[9] To be subject to government allows for disobedience when God's command contradicts a government's requirements. God continues to have first claim on people's lives.

Similarly the segment concerning civil powers in 1 Peter 2:13-17 bears a striking resemblance to Romans 13. Peter encourages unconditional love to all men but not unconditional obedience or acquiescence to any government. The absolute and perfect subjection is to God and this servanthood gives no room for wickedness. It should be instructive to us that Peter and Paul, who recommended submission to the "authorities," both died as martyrs at the hands of "kings." This fact alone speaks volumes and serves as an eloquent testimony of how the Christians understood their role in relation to the state. As "citizens of heaven" they knew that their first obligation was to conduct their lives in a manner which would match their citizenship. During the sixteenth century, Anabaptists recovered this understanding when they declared that government is "outside the perfection of Christ".[10] In the face of testing by political authorities, their highest loyalty was to Christ. "It is a good thing to be law abiding," they said, "but it is better that we be Christ-abiding."[11]

While space here does not permit us to explore differing interpretations in depth, individuals and congregations are encouraged to research the resources[12] and to discuss the implications of Christian faith for tax realities. Open-minded listening and interaction is one excellent way in which congregations can become communities of discernment. As in ancient days there is a continuing need for people who have "understanding of the times, to know what Israel ought to do" (1 Chronicles 12:32).

The Bible, coupled with Spirit-directed concern, has plenty of guidance to offer. If we invite God to speak to us through it we will have joined in the quest of "doing the truth."

New Occasions Teach New Duties

In our technological age, new implications arise from conscientious objection to war. Despite the continuing need for personnel, the development of automated weapons makes it unnecessary to engage extensive manpower to carry on a war. Furthermore, sophisticated weapons have separated military personnel from visual or other physical contact with either an enemy or with civilian victims. William Stringfellow observes,

> This extraordinary change in warfare places military professionals and citizens back home in more nearly the same practical relationship to those who are being killed. And if it is tempting to suppose that remote proximity abolishes responsibility for the killing, it must be remembered that the use of apparently anonymous automated weapons exposes the common and equal culpability for slaughter of those who pull the trigger and those who press the button with those who manufacture the means and those who pay the taxes. . . .[13]

Sophisticated weapons are the primary tool of war and these require extraordinary amounts of money.

Although a person may not be drafted into the military, he is forced, in a real way, to support it with his tax money. Consequently, the conscription (or confiscation) of money has become more important than the conscription of people. Money and materials, not people, have become the essential ingredient for today's war.

20

Vast sums of money, secured through the Internal Revenue Service, are required to purchase and maintain the enormously expensive push-button weapons. Preparation for full-scale war in our day calls for "drafted dollars" rather than "drafted persons." The federal income tax is the chief link connecting each individual's daily labor with the tremendous buildup for war.

Paying for War While Praying for Peace

If we "see life clearly and see it whole" it seems artificial to distinguish between being a military warrior and paying government for the implements of war. Is it any wonder that people are agonized by the contradictions of paying for war while praying for peace? To insist on personally abstaining from war while paying for it with taxes suggests an ethical inconsistency. To finance and pay for an activity is to participate in it.

Most Christians simultaneously affirm the legitimacy of taxation by governments and the obligation we have to pay taxes for all purposes which do not conflict with the Christian conscience. How then can we obey God and not pay taxes? Unless, of course, we are involved in the shedding of blood.[14] And there's the rub.

Getting Away with Murder

If you were handed a gun, right now, and told to shoot a man—or drop napalm on a village—you couldn't do it. . . . But the same good people who would vomit at the sight of burning flesh and blood on our hands have no qualms paying taxes for somebody else to kill and burn.

If we are forced to face the issues, we make excuses. . . . The managers of the Empire will let us speak—as long as we hand over the young men and the cash. And we are afraid to refuse. . . .

The government could never get away with murder—in Vietnam or any place—without help. The War Machine must be fed warm bodies and cold cash by the millions.[15]

That is how John E. Steen of Santa Ana, California, saw the personal responsibility each citizen shared for involvement in the Vietnam war.

The issue seemed to be just as clear during the Revolutionary War period in America. In those days John Carmichael, a Scottish Presbyterian pastor in Chester County, Pennsylvania, had little sympathy with the nonresistant sects who refused to pay war taxes, but he saw no distinction between fighting and paying the cost of war. In his 1775 sermon on Romans 13 he asserted:

> . . . if it was unlawful and anti-Christian, or anti-scriptural to support war, it would be unlawful to pay taxes; if it is unlawful to go to war, it is unlawful to pay another to do it, or to go do it.[16]

Interestingly enough Carmichael's reasoning expressed accurately the perspective of Andrew Ziegler, another Pennsylvanian of that era, who believed that collecting taxes from his Mennonite people was equivalent to "forcing nonresistant people to go to war."[17] Apart from the danger involved in war, Ziegler could see "no difference between going to war and paying the tax by which the war was supported."[18]

In the first three centuries of their movement, Christians made a decisive witness against participation in warfare. Speaking on their behalf, Origen said: "We no longer wield the sword against a nation, and we no longer learn the art of war, for we have become sons of peace through Jesus our Leader. . . ."[19] It is questionable

22

whether the Christian witness against war in our time is clear because of the willingness with which we have financed Caesar's war. We need to remember that for years, even centuries, the church has blessed wars, consecreated Crusaders, baptized blitzes, and "passed the ammunition"—all this in taxes or through special appeals for material help. But the contradictions in this lifestyle have not gone unnoticed.

Questions People Ask

We have already alluded to some of the questions which arise whenever the issue of war taxes is brought into focus. Questions are both necessary and helpful in finding answers to perplexing ethical problems. Do you find any of your questions among the following?

Is it patriotic to pay war taxes?

Are there biblical or Christian reasons for not paying taxes?

Do persons who knowingly and willingly pay taxes that support war claim to be innocent of the death and destruction that militarism inflicts upon other people?

Can a Christian in our day pay war taxes and still consider himself to be a bonafide conscientious objector to war?

Are Christians being too compliant when they obey every government demand?

Are Christians correct in challenging the right of a government to tax them for waging war?

What is the annual financial contribution which each family in North America makes toward war through taxation?

Is concern about war taxes a new issue, or is there a history of tax refusal?

Should every person, on receipt of the government's demand for money to kill, hurry as fast as he can to comply?

Should Christians take their obligations toward government more seriously than their church obligations?

Unless people dissent from paying war taxes, how are government leaders to know that Christians are opposed to making war on other peoples called "enemies"?

How can people reduce their complicity in war under present IRS regulations?

Are there people who have risked obeying God rather than the IRS?

Is there a difference between what God expects of us as individuals compared to what He expects of us when we participate in groups?

Why are church institutions so timid in the face of evil?

Does God expect us to follow the dualistic "two-kingdom ethic" with governmental demands taking precedence over our personal moral obligations?

Do we really have moral responsibility for the tax money we pay once it is in the government's treasury?

Are we accountable to both God and Caesar in equal measure?

Is there a necessary incompatibility between Christian love and paying taxes?

If participation in warfare makes me guilty of sin and if I pay taxes to the Government for military purposes, do I not share moral responsibility for the killing which the Government does in my name?

Does the proportion of government monies used for military purposes have any bearing on the Christian's general obligation to pay taxes?

If accountability is related to control and the ability to affect decisions, is it proper to hold people accountable for evil consequences over which they appear to have little or no control?

Is there clear bibical teaching that all taxes levied by government should be paid without resistance?

Do you see the conscientious objection to paying war taxes as a logical extension of being a conscientious objector to war?

Is there really no difference between performing military service and paying war-related taxes?

Would you support legislation which would enable citizens to designate a percentage of their income tax (equal to the military portion of the federal budget) to a world peace fund?

Should a church agency withhold taxes from its employees as required by law, even if more than fifty percent of the tax goes for military purposes?

Could a government ever be so unjust and murderous in its policies that you would resist paying taxes to it?

How much responsibility can the rulers assume over our consciences, and how much obedience can they rightfully demand?

Can we really accept paying taxes to support "a hospital that butchers two and heals one?"

How can we maintain our integrity as persons while giving to such diametrically opposed causes?

What constitutes faithfulness for a congregation wanting to take a position on war tax payment?

Can the Scriptures provide us with the means of testing whether or not payment of war taxes constitutes a form of idolatry?

Must we personally survive at the expense of others in our world who are less powerful?

"Suppose Caesar would level a 10 percent tax to pay for the extermination of Mennonites. Would we encourage everyone to 'render unto Caesar what he asks for'?"[20]

In God's eyes does it make a difference whose death a government asks us to pay for?

Everybody's Doing It

Human beings are often inclined to make excuses. As one maxim puts it, "Whenever you need an excuse, any excuse will do." There is good precedent for paying taxes. Furthermore, the penalties imposed for not paying taxes help to keep us sufficiently motivated. But what if we comply for the wrong reason? Are public pressures and expectations necessarily the voice of God? Are the majority decisions of elected governments infallible decisions about good and evil? Specifically, is it right for me to pay war taxes just because others are doing it?

M. Kamel Hussein focuses on such a dilemma in his dramatic interpretation of the life of Jesus, *City of Wrong: A Friday in Jerusalem*. The core theme of his book examines "the collective as man's all too frequent plea to justify wrong."[21] Somehow the greatest crimes are easily perpetrated when responsibility for those acts is distributed among many persons. A small share of the blame is hardly significant enough for the conscience to bother about. When everyone is responsible no one is responsible. Hussein contends that the crucifixon of Jesus, an obvious wrong, "was carried through by dint of being parceled out among a large number of people so that no single individual had any longer to think of

26

himself as personally responsible."[22] But communal consent is no guarantee of innocence. Here is the reason why:

Men in communities take differing attitudes from those of individuals towards right and wrong and whether to act or not to act. Communities readily do the wrong because the individuals composing them share out the weight of guilt and none of them feels personally implicated. Each thinks of his partners as exempting him from implication in that his particular share of responsibility is very slight. He argues too that even if he had not participated it would have happened anyhow. Communities as such are not readily inclined to take action for the good, because the individuals who make them up prefer to have the credit. When, however, communities abstain from their obligations toward what is good that does not absolve individuals from reproach and pangs of conscience. For then each individual feels himself culpable, not having performed his proper duty, even though he is not alone in his disinclination and his reluctance for risks.[23]

This excerpt identifies sin as "collective irresponsibility." Sin seems to disappear whenever a group of people can be made to share the responsibility for what would be a sin if an individual did it. The load of guilt rapidly lifts from the shoulders of persons when the guilt is shared. The lynching of blacks, the mass murder of Indians and Japanese by the United States, and the Nazi attempt to liquidate the Jews all serve as examples of group violence where the indivudal is less and less clearly accountable for his actions or those of his group.

Karl Menninger points out that—

No one disputes the evilness of the dreadful acts of war, but who is guilty? Not I, I obeyed orders. Not I, I merely transmitted the orders. Not I, I issued the orders on the basis of command decisions. Not I, I was only the executive of the managerial group. Not we, we specified a general objective in keeping with the national purpose.[24]

Is this the kind of sanction which makes it possible for us who are conscientiously opposed to war to keep on paying the taxes which make it possible? How can we be freed from blind obedience to those demonic powers which make Auschwitz's ovens a mere prelude to the brutality of man?

Waves of War Tax Concern

War tax anxiety, long buried in history, is coming to life again. Looking at 460 years of Anabaptist history it appears that there were three major waves of concern: (1) among the Hutterites of the sixteenth century who courageously put word and deed together at great risk to their own lives; (2) among the Brethren, Quakers, Mennonites, Moravians, and Schwenkfelders of Colonial America who despite the risks of disloyalty were committed not to offend God or their consciences; and (3) among people of North America who, out of the agony of war during the past two decades, have come to recognize the inconsistency of praying for peace while paying for war.

War has a way of bringing out the best as well as the worst in human beings. Because it is a crisis experience for the people involved, such situations have created opportunities for growth in following Jesus. They have also revealed the shallowness of much Christian commitment. Fortunately the vision is not limited to those who call themselves Christian. The following items help put the "taxes for war" issue in historical perspective.[25]

Blood Money and Protection Refused

The Hutterites of the sixteenth century took a strong position against what they termed "blood money." They consistently refused to pay war taxes and special levies. In 1545 Peter Riedemann wrote:

> For war, killing, and bloodshed (where it is demanded especially for that) we give nothing, but not out of wickedness or artibrariness, but out of the fear of God (1 Timothy 5) that we may not be partakers in strange sins.[26]

Claus Felbinger, another Hutterite brother, confirmed this perspective in a written confession of 1560:

> Therefore we are gladly and willingly subject to the government for the Lord's sake, and in all just matters we will in no way oppose it. When, however, the government requires of us what is contrary to our faith and conscience—as swearing oaths and paying hangman's dues or taxes for war—then we do not obey its command. This we do not out of obstinancy or pride, but only out of pure fear of God. For it is our duty to obey God rather than men (Acts 5:29).[27]

Felbinger and a partner were beheaded on July 19, 1560. Their witness was clear and unequivocal. Despite intense pressure and considerable hardship, the Hutterite witness continued well into the nineteenth and twentieth centuries. Some Anabaptists did not have as strong a position on this issue. There was disagreement among several groups in Europe.

One of the clearest and most appropriate instances of war tax refusal in North America took place in 1637 when the relatively peaceable Algonquin Indians opposed taxation for armaments by the Dutch. After having sold arms to the Iroquis Indians, William Kieft tried to pacify the offended Algonquins by improving Fort Amsterdam which he claimed was to provide protection for Algonquins as well as for the Dutch settlers. When he sent his tax collectors to the Indians they were met with a storm of resistance: "Protection indeed! His fort was no protection to them. They had not asked to build it, and were not going to help maintain it."[28]

A Potent Witness for Peace

The American Quakers made refusal of war taxes an integral part of what was undoubtedly one of the most potent witnesses for peace and against war in any age by any people. As early as 1711 William Penn informed the Queen of England that his conscience would not allow "a tribute to carry on any war, nor ought true Christians to pay it."[29] Then in 1715 an anonymous Quaker argued with even greater certainty in a pamphlet entitled *Tribute to Caesar.*

> To pay ordinary taxes is justifiable, of course, and it is not always necessary to inquire what the government does with them. But when taxes are levied specifically for war purposes, and announced as such, the Christian must refuse to pay them, says the author. Hence the expedient of voting money "for the queen's use" in response to a demand for military aid is a sacrifice of principle.[30]

Tax refusal as a moral protest against war was already practiced by the Quaker assembly of the Colony of Pennsylvania in 1709. They refused to grant the £4,000 which was requested by the English Crown for an expedition into Canada, but voted to give £500 to the queen as a token of respect, provided that "the money should be put into a safe hand till they were satisfied from England it would not be employed in use of war. . . ."[31]

John Woolman (1720-72) admitted that he had longstanding scruples against paying taxes "for carrying on wars." He could see no effective difference between actually fighting a war and supporting it with taxes. In his *Journal*, he wrote:

> To refuse the active payment of a tax which our society generally paid was exceeding disagreeable, but to do a thing contrary to my conscience appeared yet more dreadful. . . . Thus, by small degrees, we might approach so near to fighting that the distinction would be little else but the name of a peaceable people.[32]

The tax resistance movement was given good footing in 1755 when Dunkards (Church of the Brethren) and Quakers refused to pay taxes for the French and Indian campaigns of the Seven Years' War.[33] During that military conflict, the Quakers—John Woolman, Anthony Benezet, and John Churchman—led a protest movement against passage of a tax bill that included provisions for killing Indians. After the "militia bill" was passed (November, 1755), they refused to pay their taxes "though suffering be the consequence of refusal." Twenty-one years later, one of the tests of a Quaker's sincerity was his refusal to pay taxes for the Revolutionary War.[34]

All Civic Obligations—Save One
The nonresistant sects fulfilled all civic obligations—save one. They were not willing to participate in war either bodily or through financial contributions. They claimed indulgence on no other point. One patriot lamented the lack of cooperation received from the Dunkards:

31

They refused in the most positive manner to pay a dollar to support those who were willing to take up arms to defend their homes and their firesides . . . they were *non-resistants!* They might, at least, have furnished money, for they always had an abundance of that, the hoarding of which seemed to be the sole aim and object of life with them. But, no; not a dollar![35]

Unfortunately when money was given, the authorities understood their voluntary contributions "for the needy" as donations to the war chest. It did not matter where Quakers, Mennonites, or Brethren lived, the problem of paying for war soon caught up with them. Not infrequently questions arose from the war on which they could not all agree. The expulsion of Bishop Christian Funk in 1777 was a result of this debate over the propriety of paying Congressional war taxes.[36] Funk had taken the position in favor of payment.

On November 7, 1775, Mennonites and Church of the Brethren people submitted a joint declaration to the General Assembly of the Commonwealth of Pennsylvania. In that petition the Dunkards and Mennonites said they were ready at all times to help those in need or distress—

—it being our Principle to feed the Hungry and give the Thirsty Drink;—we have dedicated ourselves to serve all Men in every Thing that can be helpful to the Preservation of Men's lives; but we find no Freedom in giving, or doing, or assisting in any Thing by which Men's Lives are destroyed or hurt.[37]

The Faithful Church in a Hostile World

In Prussia both military and church taxes were based on land ownership. Mennonites were disinclined to pay for the support of either the military or the state church. By the 1780s they were apprehensive about the growing military preparations, particularly the annual tax of 5,000 thaler required for the support of military schools. This factor prompted many to relocate in southern Russia.[38]

Klass Reimer, a Mennonite minister of Danzig and later of Molotschna in Russia (1805 f.), "was opposed to contributions made to the Russian government during the Napoleonic War."[39] He was appalled at the lack of personal morality and ethical concern among the Mennonites. To promote his concern for the restoration of an authentic biblical-Anabaptist Christianity, he began meeting with like-minded Christians in 1812, and by 1814 they were organized as a separate group (the "Kleine Gemeinde").

Caught Between Two Fires

Perhaps one of the severest tests to which peace principles were ever put occurred in Ireland during the rebellion of 1798. During that terrible conflict, the Irish Quakers were continually caught between two fires. The Protestant faction viewed them with suspicion because they refused to fight or to pay military taxes, and the insurgents thought they should be killed because they would neither profess belief in the Catholic religion nor help them fight for Irish freedom.[40]

Difficult as it was to meet public hostility, Quakers and the Brethren did not hesitate to exercise discipline on those who failed to follow the historic peace teaching of the church. By and large Mennonite opposition to war taxes was not as intense as that of the Quakers. What agonizing predicaments the conscientious objectors found themselves in, for they were punished by the state if they did not support war efforts and by the church if they did!

The Shakers in New Hampshire, a people that tried to remake society, were not as ambivalent as Mennonites about their response to the demands of war. In 1818 they addressed the Legislature in the following terms:

> Anything then of the coercive nature, under whatever name, practised against conscience, must be a pointed violation of these rights. . . .
> And should we consent to pay a tax as an equivalent this would be a virtual acknowledgement that the liberty of conscience is not our natural right; but may be purchased at a stated price.
> Such a concession involves in it, a principle derogatory to the Almighty, because it requires us to purchase of government, liberty to serve God with our persons, at the expense of sinning against him with our property.
> . . . we feel ourselves impelled by the most sacred obligations of duty, to decline . . . let the consequences be what they may.[41]

An Influential Night in Prison

The United States war against Mexico in 1846 is important to our review because it and the Massachusetts poll tax provoked Henry David Thoreau to write his famous essay on civil disobedience.[42] Thoreau's essay is a justification for opposing the state when law and conscience conflict. He tried to give encouragement to timid persons who held social justice concerns but who did not dare to say "no"—did not dare to disobey the government that perpetuated evils which they deplored. Because Thoreau viewed slavery as an unmitigated evil he rejected the war and refused to pay the tax levied to support it. Rejecting the assumption that the citizen must support all governmental activities, even those which fall short of being just, he asserted that government "can have no pure right over my person and property but what I concede to it." Consequently he decided for himself that certain taxes were morally justified and that certain others were not. For him the refusal to pay taxes was an effort to use his "whole influence" to stop "a violent and bloody measure." There will never be a really free state, he said, "until the state comes to recognize the individual as a higher and independent power, from which all its own power and authority are derived, and treats him accordingly." Furthermore it was his conviction that "if in a country the government acts wrongly, then a prison is the only place a self-respecting citizen can live in."[43] Considering his impact upon millions of people through Tolstoy, Gandhi, and Martin Luther King, Jr., his individual witness was obviously profound.

Leo Tolstoy (1828-1910), deeply impressed by the Sermon on the Mount, understood conscientious objection to war to include the problem of war taxes.

"You may wish to make me a participator in murder; you demand of me money for the preparation of weapons; and want me to take part in the organized assembly of murderers;" says the reasonable man—he who has neither sold nor obscured his conscience. "But I profess that law— the same that is also professed by you—which long ago forbade not murder only, but all hostility also, and therefore I cannot obey you."[44]

Your Money or Your Life!

By the time of the Civil War, the Quakers were still vigorously protesting war taxes, but the Brethren and the

35

Mennonites were more inclined to pay whatever the government required of them. Of course, there were individual protests such as the one made by a Quaker named Maule who became concerned over the lax spiritual condition of many of his friends who were not disturbed by taxes levied for war purposes. He refused to pay the County Treasurer 8½ percent of the tax for 1861, "which was the part expressly named in the tax list as for the war at that time."[45]

During the American Civil War both systems of national conscription offered two alternatives to pacifists. Exemption from the draft could be obtained either by furnishing an acceptable substitute or by paying $300 ($500 in the South) for hiring one. There was considerable opposition to this arrangement among the conscientious objectors because the only way of securing exemption was to hire a substitute, either directly or indirectly. And it did not seem consistent to hire another person to do that which one could not conscientiously do oneself.[46]

"To Pay an Onerous Tax"

At the time that Mennonites were migrating to Kansas an existing law (1865) required the payment of a thirty-dollar fine payable each May for the privilege of exemption from military service. Apparently Governor Osborne saw this as an infringement on the citizen's freedom and as a disadvantage in securing Mennonite immigrants for Kansas. On January 15, 1874, he proposed an amendment to the existing law. The governor said:

It is hoped that large accessions may be made of these worthy settlers, and it may properly be considered whether any class of people who are conscientiously opposed to bear-

36

ing arms should be compelled to pay an onerous tax to be relieved therefrom. It strikes me as incongruous that such religious convictions should be taxable by our laws.[47]

In response to the governor's recommendations, the legislature repealed the "onerous tax" on March 9, 1874.

"Justified in Giving Neither Money nor Soldiers"
The Vyborg Manifesto of July 23, 1906, gave the people of Russia new freedom. Having dissolved the government it declared that the populace was "justified in giving neither money nor soldiers."[48] Years later the triumph of the Bolsheviks in October of 1917 produced a reign of terror for the Mennonites. Despite attempts to remain nonresistant and loving the struggle for survival resulted in desperate measures. Mennonite young people yielded to the spirit of militarism and organized the Self-Defense Corps. This proved to be not only a tactical blunder but also a gross violation of historic biblical faith.[49] In this episode some Mennonites obviously financed war preparations. Among the Dutch Mennonites practically all opposition to war was gone by 1900. Having become respectable and wealthy in their society they suffered a loss of vitality and a serious decline in membership (200,000 to 30,000). It is reported that "they won the good will of the state on several occasions by making very substantial contributions in money when their country was at war."[50]

World War I—A Watershed Experience
For Mennonites, World War I was a severe test of their Christian faith. As their most profound civic identity crisis in America, it proved to be a turning point in their

history. According to James C. Juhnke, a Mennonite historian, the leading issues in the confrontation between the nonresistant Mennonites and the crusading Americans were "military service, the war bond drives, and the German language." They cooperated with patriotic expectations as best they could, "developing their own programs of voluntary benevolence and relief to provide a moral equivalent of military service and war bond drives."[51] At the beginning it was generally agreed among the Mennonite leadership that participation in the war effort through the purchasing of bonds was wrong. But with increased pressure practically everyone "bought a few bonds." Bond drives were designed not only to finance the war but also to foster patriotism. Margaret Entz described the results of this in Kansas as follows:

Refusal to buy war bonds was one of the standards by which the American patriotic community judged the Mennonites to be unworthy of their citizenship. Bonds were not only of monetary value, they also symbolized patriotic support of American's war effort along with her ideals of democracy and liberty. By attaching these values to the Liberty Loans, the Treasury Department succeeded remarkably in selling bonds. In light of the fact that the war economy was not a matter of consumer choice and was imposed upon people involuntarily, this achievement was even more notable. Necessary war financing was done through voluntary means in order to gain the support of the American people, but with demanding methods that necessitated compliance from all.

Mennonites were caught in this contradictory government policy. If bonds were truly voluntary, then purchasing them was an intentional contribution to a cause the Mennonites abhorred. However, the Treasury Department undermined the principle of voluntarism by urging the necessity of bond purchases on the local level. Mennonites were scorned, intimidated, threatened, and physically harmed until they bought bonds. The war that failed miserably to make the world safe for democracy, also failed to perpetuate democracy at home.[52]

To Pay or Not to Pay, That Is the Question

To illustrate the consequences of the government's World War I strategy we mention three peacemaking incidents from that period.

John Schrag, a farmer from rural Burrton, Kansas, became the victim of mob violence on November 11, 1918, when he was forced to buy war bonds or bear the consequences. He was beaten, smeared with yellow paint, imprisoned, and taken to court for disrespect to the American flag. Despite the unforgettable jolt, he could not support the war and hate Germany. Years later, Charles Gordon, a member of that mob testified to Schrag's calmness throughout the ordeal: "He exemplified the life of Christ more than any man I ever saw in my life."[53]

Another encounter with zealous patriots took place near Bloomfield, Montana, where Pastor John Franz and members of the Bethlehem congregation were criticized for their refusal to take part in the war. Specifically, they were asked why they refused to buy war bonds. In responding to this challenge Pastor Franz tried to explain that—

Christians really own nothing. We are here to take care of all God's things. Since our money is God's money, we can use it only for things that please Him. We cannot buy war bonds, because that makes war possible. Using our money to make it possible for others to be killed would be just as wrong as going into the army and killing a man ourselves.[54]

Several years later one of the twelve men who had tried to hang Pastor Franz stopped to ask him a sober question: "Will you forgive me for the great wrong I did to you and to your family?"

In keeping with their belief in the necessity of civil government, Hutterites pay all taxes levied against them except war taxes. The latter are refused in obedience to the lordship of Christ.[55] Although willing to contribute money for the relief of war sufferers, the Hutterites in South Dakota refused to purchase Liberty Bonds. Most also refused to contribute to the Red Cross.

> When a local bond committee assigned the Hutterites a quota, and they refused to buy any bonds, a group of patriotic enthusiasts visited the Jamesville colony and without opposition drove away a hundred steers and a thousand sheep. They were shipped to the livestock market, the proceeds to be invested in war bonds. The packing houses, however, refused to take the stolen cattle, and they had to be sold at auction in Yankton for about half of their value.[55]

All three of the above accounts remind us of the need for creative imagination in applying the gospel, courage to endure persecution and suffering, and deep commitment to implement faithfully the way of the cross. A moving hymn suggests the nature of the conflict:

> Once to every man and nation comes the moment to decide,
> In the strife of Truth with Falsehood, for the good or evil side. . . .
> New occasions teach new duties, Time makes ancient good uncouth;

They must upward still, and onward, who would keep
abreast of Truth. . . .
Though the cause of evil prosper, yet 'tis truth alone is
strong.
Though her portion be the scaffold, and upon the throne be
wrong,
Yet that scaffold sways the future, and, behind the dim
unknown
Standeth God within the shadow keeping watch above His
own.[56]

Strong Decisions, Careful Citizens

The "Merchants of Death" debate raged through the
1930s. In 1933 a query on protesting against military
taxes was brought to the annual Church of the Brethren
Conference. It was answered the following year by a
report from the Board of Christian Education which
listed several methods of protest but not including the
refusal of payment.[57] Apparently this possibility did not
enter the minds either of those bringing the query, the
Board that formulated the answer, or the conference that
adopted it. With the exception of the 1781 minute that
allows tax refusal as a conscientious possibility, it was not
until 1968, the peak of the Vietnam War, that any of the
church's many statements on war as much as took note of
the matter. In that year the revision of the original 1948
statement on war added a significant section on "The
Church and Taxes for War Purposes."

For the most part the war tax issue remained dormant
during World War II. Among the first of the Mennonites
to mention the subject was a nonregistrant, Austin
Regier, who was sentenced to one year and one day in
federal penitentiary for refusing to comply with the
draft. Firmly committed to the way of love and indi-

41

vidual responsibility, he believed that "the consistent pacifist should refuse war taxes."[58]

Peace Agitator

A. J. Muste (1875-1967) was regarded by many as the outstanding spokesman in the United States for the Christian pacifist position. As early as 1936 it was his conviction that the most effective thing which people in the world could do was "to dissociate themselves completely from war." Muste worked energetically with the war tax problem, refusing from 1948 on to pay Federal income taxes. Not until 1951 was he questioned by Internal Revenue agents, and not until 1960 was he brought into court. Whenever there was opportunity he articulated the position that there should be alternatives to making H-bombs or paying for making them. He repeatedly challenged the right of the government to tax him for waging war. From his perspective,

> . . . the two decisive powers of government with respect to war are the power to conscript and the power to tax. In regard to the second I have come to the conviction that I am at least in conscience bound to challenge the right of the government to tax me for waging war, and in particular for the production of atomic and bacterial weapons.[59]

The Peacemaker Movement

The idea of organizing war tax resistance in this country seems to have begun with the Peacemaker Movement which was formed by 250 pacifists in Chicago early in 1948. This heterogenous group of Americans are united by their refusal to pay taxes so long as the federal budget is weighted so heavily by military expenditures. Since coming together they have been saying "no" to conscription for war and making the alternatives known to others through their publication, *The Peacemaker.* Since February 1963, the Movement has also published a useful *Handbook on Nonpayment of War Taxes* which contains alternative suggestions and numerous personal histories.[60]

An update on the Peacemaker witness is pertinent. In 1975 the Internal Revenue Service discovered itself in a "no win" position and subsequently returned to Gano Peacemakers, Inc., the house near Cincinnati which had been seized by the IRS earlier. This experience confirmed for Ernest and Marion Bromley, former editors of *The Peacemaker,* the knowledge that the authorities of death are *not* all-powerful. For the Bromleys there is no reason to fear the IRS. Mrs. Bromley reported:

> One of the pleasant feelings we have about the reversal of the sale (besides knowing that we can continue to live on these two acres) is that many people have told us they got a real lift when they heard that some "little people" had prevailed in the struggle with the IRS. We had the feeling that our daily leafleting and constant public statements during the seven months' campaign had, at least, the effect of showing that people need not *fear* this government agency. People do fear the IRS and that is an unworthy attitude. What can they take away that is of real value?[61]

Confronting Congress and the IRS

One of the leading peace movements of the past fifty years is the War Resisters League. Since its inception in 1923, the League has sought to create a just and peaceful society through nonviolet and life-supporting methods. Jessie Wallace Hughan, one of WRL's founders, articulated its first policy on war taxes in a 1935 pamphlet. Although she didn't advocate resistance at that time, she urged taxpayers to consider "taxation as a form of seizure, not a voluntary contribution." War tax refusal has been an ongoing activity of the League since the 1940s. By 1953 demonstrations at IRS Centers were being held. The first WRL call for total tax resistance was issued in 1957. Marion Bromley, a League member and one of the founders of Peacemakers, wrote:

> War resisters pledge they "will not support any kind of war." If we have reached the point where the major "support" that is demanded is financial, is it not time to break ranks, to bring the deed more nearly into harmony with the pledge?[62]

From that point on, the League considered tax resistance a basic, if not central, part of its program. One of the movement's most joyous occasions took place in 1969 when resisters formed War Tax Resistance, a new and distinct organization whose activities would focus solely on all aspects of tax refusal. Working with vigor and imagination the movement has moved into new forms of resistance activity such as court appeals for employee rights against the withholding of war taxes. The League's confrontation with the Internal Revenue Service in 1974 resulted in the seizure by IRS of $3,432.58 from its bank account. This experience confirmed the need for a continuing protest despite the hassles and the risks. *Liberation* magazine, begun in 1956, and *Win*, begun in 1965, are two effective instruments for propagating nonviolent insights and the astounding costs of militarism.

Similar to the WRL is the Central Committee for Conscientious Objectors which began in Philadelphia in mid-1948 to deal with conscription issues. By 1956, realizing that conscientious objection relates not only to the draft but to all conflicts between the state and moral choice, CCCO extended its services to objectors to include tax payments for war purposes. The Milton Mayer Defense Fund to reclaim war taxes was one of their primary accomplishments during the 1950s. In the 1960s a number of staff members were tax resisters. CCCO policy has always been to refuse to honor IRS levies so as not to become a collection agency for the IRS. In 1978 for the first time, IRS has brought suit against CCCO for their failure to pay the tax debt allegedly owed by a past employee who has refused for reasons of conscience. Steven Gulick bases his position on the Quaker teaching that one should not support war or preparations for war.[63]

Would Jesus Pay for Atom Bombs?

Two of the key figures in the anti-war tax movement have been deeply concerned about the poor in our society. They are Ammon Hennacy (1893-1970) and Dorothy Day (1897-   ). Both of these forceful leaders have been actively involved in the Hospitality Houses operated by the Catholic Worker Movement. Catholic opposition to war has taken on new significance since the founding of the movement in 1933. In January of 1942, Dorothy Day wrote to her fellow workers:

> We are still pacifists. Our manifesto is the Sermon on the Mount, which means that we will try to be peacemakers. . . . We will not participate in armed warfare or in making munitions, or by buying government bonds to prosecute the war, or in urging others to these efforts.[64]

More recently she declared:

> Working for a better order here in this world means a terrible struggle. . . . Our means are prayer and fasting, and the nonpayment of federal income tax which goes to war.[65]

Bernard Survil of Indianapolis, Indiana, has been part of a group called Ammon's Tax Associates since the early 1970s. As a Roman Catholic priest he has brought together a group of concerned persons who are committed to the study and practice of war tax objection. They urge churches to help legitimize war tax objection as a moral alternative to war. In 1971 they submitted a 7-page "Plea for Support" to the American Bishop representatives to the Roman Synod. Ammon's Tax Associates sense that an individual may make a conscientious decision to withhold war taxes when three elements concur:

> (1) He has enough specific information which he accepts as true with a sufficiently high degree of confidence.
> (2) He experiences the moral imperative to act upon this information in this individual way, after weighing the matters of moral integrity, the usefulness or effectiveness of the act in accomplishing its purposes, as well as considering the accompanying effects not willed directly but which will most likely follow from the decision.
> (3) The courage (or foolhardiness) to go through with it.[66]

The reason war tax objection is so rare is that few people can honestly say that they feel informed enough to move beyond step 1. Many persons could be moved from indecision to action by increasing their awareness of the issue and its implications.

A Call to Action Conference held in Detroit recommended that the Catholic Church—

46

. . . give its support to those who on grounds of conscience refuse to serve in war or preparation for war; that Catholics support legal provision for selective and general conscientious objection to military service and to the payment of war or military taxes.[67]

Among the more militant leaders of the Catholic war resistance movement are Daniel and Philip Berrigan, David Miller, and Tom Cornell, all of whom have been convicted in federal courts for acts growing out of their religious objection to the war system.

During the past two decades, Brethren, Quakers, Mennonites, and others have become increasingly disturbed over the large portion of tax monies which contribute so heavily to finance past, present, and future wars. It has been calculated that out of a 12-month tax period the United States taxpayer works nearly six months before his federal income tax has paid for anything beyond current military expenses and the cost of past wars.[68] Out of this awareness new statements have been issued.[69] From the wealth of material available we quote only one sampling:

> The levying of war taxes is another form of conscription which, along with the conscription of manpower, makes war possible. We are accountable to God for the use of our financial resources and should protest the use of our taxes in the promotion and waging of war. We stand by those who feel called to resist the payment of that portion of taxes being used for military purposes.[70]

In response to the growing war tax concern, the Commission on Home Ministries of the General Conference Mennonite Church began publishing the *God and Caesar* newsletter in January of 1975. The mailing list has grown dramatically.[71] Peaceful tax paying is already a worldwide movement. Japanese leaders have experienced considerable support for a better way.[72] Thousands in the United States have declined to pay the federal telephone excise tax since 1966, including a few Mennonite and Church of the Brethren congregations. Most of these are seeking alternative uses for these funds. Legal research has been done by the Peacemaker Movement and the American Friends Service Committee.[73]

While there is this serious reexamination of the war tax issue, it must be remembered that many see no inconsistency between a commitment to Christian love and the payment of war taxes. Because of this diversity there is a need to cultivate a spirit of discernment where people are loved whether or not they agree with one another's approach to this ethical dilemma.

Too Much to Caesar, Too Little to God?

The annual United States budget is dominated by a hydra-headed military appropriation. The costs of technological weaponry are astronomical. And the amount Christians pay for things they know are absolutely evil is frightening. In 1959 it was estimated that the average American family paid $850 per year for military defense through taxes.[74] For fiscal 1977 it was estimated that "the average American family is taxed $1,600 annually to support the military program of a government that gave us Watergate, Vietnam, the CIA, and the largest nuclear stockpile in the world."[75] It should be no secret to anyone that Christians today pay more in taxes for the support of the military than they give voluntarily for the support of the church and other benevolent causes. Does this constitute defensible stewardship? Not if money

48

represents something of our life energy. Can people really believe that they are advancing the cause of Christ when they hand over more money to pay for war than they give to heal the wounds of the world? Schizophrenic giving describes it best. War taxes are a tremendous waste of resources. They are in fact a theft from those who hunger and are not fed, those who are cold and not clothed. The militaristic budget of death reveals that stewardship is a fearfully neglected aspect of the gospel in our time.[76]

Killing Via the Tax Method

In view of the increased sensitivity about the business of paying for war let us identify two of the ways in which citizens are implicated in war taxes.

1. The excise tax on telephone service is the most explicit tax for war in the United States. It has been associated with war spending since 1914. It was reinstated in 1966 to help pay for the Vietnam war. Congressman Wilbur Mills said, "It is clear that the Vietnam operation and only the Vietnam operation makes this bill necessary."[77] And Senator Frank Church confirmed that "when all the rhetoric is stripped away (this added tax) is simply a war tax."[78] "That last phone bill was a real killer!" the posters stated. No fooling. The Federal excise tax has helped to make certain that thousands of people will never use the telephone.

2. The Federal income tax and particularly the system of withholding income at the source provide funds for war. Defense spending in the United States has escalated to 40 and 70 percent of the national budget. The money for this budget of death is conscripted through the federal income tax—the chief link connecting each indi-

49

vidual's daily labor with the continuing buildup for war. It is absolutely frightening to contemplate the enormous sums of money which Christians have been paying for war. With one hand we give generously for life-building purposes, and with the other we cancel out the good that we have done by allowing the secular power to conscript an even larger amount of money for the destruction of human life. Who will deliver us from this death—from rendering unto Caesar that which is not his?

The federal income tax became possible in 1913 when the sixteenth amendment to the Constitution was adopted. Prior to that time the Supreme Court frequently challenged the constitutionality of revenue acts. It is believed that the Civil War (1861-65) accelerated the development of income taxation. The first income tax in the United States was imposed under Lincoln in 1862 when the costs of the Civil War were resulting in an increase of the public debt by as much as two million dollars per day. The tax was abolished ten years later.

The withholding system of tax collection in the United States first became law in June 1943. At that time only 10 percent of the population paid income taxes. The shift from a "class tax" to a "pay-as-you-earn mass tax" was necessitated by the tremendous cost of weapons during World War II. Two fifths of the total cost of the war was paid for out of these taxes, and the number of persons liable was raised between 1939 and 1943 from four to thirty million. Through this indirect method of withholding the government enforces collection through employers who are the unsalaried agents of the Internal Revenue Service. In reality the withholding tax is legal confiscation at the source of income for every employed citizen (with few exceptions). This arrangement undermines responsibility and makes it very difficult for the average citizen to exercise control over a portion of his own salary. In our time it seems almost natural for us to open our pocketbooks and checkbooks to every official demand of the State. Yet this was not true in the United States prior to 1913.

Signs of Hope in a Warring World

The Society of Friends, the Church of the Brethren, and more recently the Mennonites have invested time and energy urging the United States government to provide a nonmilitary arrangement for meeting tax obligations. For centuries peace church members have paid military taxes even though they refused to bear arms themselves.

Now, as the artificiality of the distinction between arms and paying for others to bear them has become so shockingly clear, more and more of our members are refusing to pay some or all of the taxes that support the military budget. . . . Many are now finding this choice so intolerable that they, as well as many tax resisters, are working for legislation which would give taxpayers who are conscientious objectors the same kind of consideration that has traditionally been given to draftees who are conscientious objectors.[79]

Two plans deserve special mention:

(1) *The Civilian Income Tax Fund.* During the early 1960s the Pacific Yearly Meeting of Friends circulated a proposed bill offering a tax alternative. Conscientious objectors would have designated their tax money for the support of the United Nations International Children's Emergency Fund (UNICEF). Some were offering to pay an additional 5 percent above their normally computed

51

tax as a proof of their sincerity. The Church of the Brethren was urging the formation of specific non-military accounts to overcome the problem of a common treasury. It was assumed that unless citizens can vote for peace as well as war with their money we still have "taxation without representation" 200 years after Independence.

(2) *The World Peace Tax Fund Act.* In a further effort to channel tax money into life-sustaining programs rather than into weapons of death, the World Peace Tax Fund Act was introduced in the House of Representatives in April 1972. It has been reintroduced annually since then as well as introduced in the Senate in 1977. If enacted the bill would establish a special trust fund and thus allow the military portion of federal taxes to be used for peaceful purposes.

The WPTF effort to obtain a legal alternative began in 1971 with a group of concerned citizens in Ann Arbor, Michigan, including some from the University of Michigan law school. For the sake of their own integrity they wanted to be freed from the requirement to kill anyone through any means, including taxation. Their purpose was to allow the citizen to redirect his taxes, not avoid them.

A National Council for a World Peace Tax Fund was organized in 1975 to promote the enactment of legislation which would grant people a legal alternative to the payment of war taxes. "Taxes for Peace Not War" is their slogan. It is doubtful that this goal will be achieved easily but there are indicators that it is a realistic one. If sufficient support develops in each state and people take the initiative to inform their congresspersons of the need for this act, the desired legislation could become law. The

Act would have great appeal to all those who feel that they are being penalized when they follow their own consciences because they are forced by law to finance multibillion dollar weapons programs. Not only would this Act give citizens the choice of voting for peace or for war, it would also help us to preserve the freedoms which the Constitution and the Bill of Rights attempt to guarantee. The idea of giving citizens tax relief for their conscientious objections to war is likely to be around for a long time.

A Peace Tax Has Its Limits

The World Peace Tax Fund Act is not an unmixed blessing. Phil M. Shenk has done a remarkable service in warning that the WPTF may not be the most faithful response to a warmongering world. He asks whether the legitimization of objection to war would strengthen the protest or whether it would mortally wound personal conviction and severely weaken social impact. Whenever the state claims to respect the consciences of those persons opposing war, Shenk feels it tends to dilute the church's prophetic voice against the world's ungodly love for war. The early church was seduced in this way by the Roman emperor Constantine's legalization of the church. Its strength was sapped, its faith made tolerant by tolerance. Special niches and legal exemptions tended to foster reclusive passivity.

Would the legal alternative in the WPTF be more responsible than tax resistance? Shenk is doubtful. He believes the church's faithful response should include both positive action and negative protest. In other words, church members can protest by refusing to pay war taxes and at the same time promote peace positively by giving time and money to peace projects. Both dimensions are necessary for a balanced peace agenda. Phil Shenk contends that the church necessarily confronts a world at odds with its values. In contrast to military budgets the church upholds a value system founded on the love of Christ. Consequently,

> . . . worldly priorities must be objected to in word and deed. If the objecting deeds are performed legally, they register little if any protest. If consciously illegal, they register an unequivocal refusal to agree with world's values. The latter gets the attention of the state, the former does not.
>
> Simple tax resistance would free the church to spend its energies calling the whole world to salvation rather than saving just itself.
>
> The church's "in-ness" but "not-of-ness" demands that it be actively concerned about the nonchurched world. Christ as Lord is subject to no other authority. Because of this, the church's most crucial task is to prophetically and faithfully enact and promote Christ's values in life without regard for political limitations or definitions. The politics of Jesus are not those of compromise, but those of dogged, active, and consistent faithfulness.[80]

For this reason MCC Peace Section recommends that people continue to work toward reduction of military spending, not resting content with special war tax exemption privileges. Any resistance to war and to those authorities which bring about war is not a negative presence. The fact is that every no implies a yes, and this *no* to killing and death can be a *yes* to healing and life. War tax resistance is a process filled with hope. It can curb the expansion of the military. While radical tax resistance may be a more courageous response than working for a special fund devoted to nonmilitary purposes, should we not welcome every effort which seeks to be faithful to the self-giving love of God revealed in Christ?

For Those Who Like a Challenge
Paying taxes is a deeply ingrained habit in the lives of most American citizens. In spite of our inclination to be tax-paying, law-abiding citizens, and despite the complexity of the war tax issue we do not need to be helpless in the face of this evil. Each of us has viable options which we can use to register our faithfulness to Jesus Christ as Lord and our opposition to corporate war making by the state within which we live. Following are methods which persons are using to say "no" to war taxes, and "yes" to taxes for peace:

(1) Engage people in conversation on this issue wherever you go and employ all legal means available to correct the injustice of war tax demands.

Paul Leatherman of Pennsylvania is a prime example of a Christian who energetically and cheerfully reaches out to persons to explore war tax options. God has given him a love for people and he welcomes every opportunity to build support for his deep ethical concern about human life. To achieve this objective he engages IRS representatives in conversation and invites them to eat meals with his family.

Are we inclined to overlook the power of persuasion which God has given to each of us? Yet every significant idea or conviction which people hold had a small beginning. The same is true for the war tax issue. Seeds of concern or awareness planted three or four decades ago have taken root and resulted in alternative movements. With imagination and persistence it might well be that a

Tax Fund for Peace could be developed. If citizens distribute leaflets, write letters to newspapers, and speak forth for new possibilities, our goal could become a reality. The separation of church and state does not mean that Christians have nothing to say to, or ask of, the state, but rather that the state cannot ask everything of them. We need not be afraid to ask for religious liberty even when we think that the powers that be are disinclined to grant it. Let us use the power of the written and spoken word. (See Appendix D).

(2) *Discontinue the voluntary payment of the federal excise tax on telephone service.* In 1966 this tax, as explicitly a war tax as any that United States citizens are asked to pay, was raised to 10 percent primarily to help pay for the war costs in Vietnam. Those who have chosen to resist the payment of war taxes have found the withholding of funds to be a simple, direct, and an effective way of letting government leaders know how they feel. At the height of resistance to the Indochina War, it was estimated there were 200,000 telephone tax resisters. Because telephone companies are not happy serving as tax collecting agents for the government they frequently give citizens support in their opposition to the tax. The tax, although small in comparison to the federal income tax, does give people a handle whereby they can be heard within a democratic structure.

At the present time it is easy to determine the amount of money which goes for the tax on the monthly telephone bill. It is designated as "U.S. Tax." People who deduct the amount from their payment generally include a postcard or letter to the telephone company along with their check or money order. Periodically, they also inform the Internal Revenue Service of the reasons behind their action. One note reads as follows:

> I do not support the priorities of our government which emphasize arms buildup at the expense of human needs. Therefore, I have deducted from my telephone bill the $_____ federal tax.
> The federal excise tax on phone service has been raised and lowered periodically since World War II depending on our country's military involvement. This war tax represents a continuing reliance on military force to protect American corporate interests abroad and therefore I can not in good conscience pay for it.[81]

Generally the risk of refusing is small even though the IRS does speak about substantial fine and prison penalties. It seems that the IRS does not want the publicity which develops when people are arrested for refusing to pay this war tax. David H. Janzen of Newton, Kansas, discovered the witness potential of this appraoch in 1972 when friends rallied to his support at the IRS's public auction of his automobile.[82] Telephone tax refusal is a small act in which money talks. It can provide a clear demonstration to people and to governments that Christians are indeed serious about following Jesus.

(3) *Increase your contributions for missions and service (tax deductible causes).* The IRS code of the United States government does permit citizens the option of giving up to 30 percent and sometimes even 50 percent of their income to charitable purposes. This means in effect that people can reduce their taxable income by increasing their giving.

Levi Keidel is convinced, however, that Mennonites today build their lifestyles around selected parts of their heritage (i.e., holy living, evangelism, voluntary poverty, or nonviolence) and thereby seriously erode the credibility of their Christian witness to people. To illustrate, Keidel writes:

> . . . We Mennonites who have set our affection upon things of earth, relished the pleasures and the conveniences of affluence, amassed material wealth like everyone else, now say that we will refuse to pay income tax as our peace witness to government. We are selecting to apply the principle of nonparticipation in violence, but not of self-imposed poverty for the sake of the kingdom of heaven.[83]

Most Christians fail to reach the standard of a tithe in their giving. In this respect refusing to pay war taxes has proven to be a blessing for many people and for many church-related causes. Attempts to make a living without being subject to war taxes have resulted in some people finding or backing into a simple lifestyle.[84] It has helped them to reorder their priorities. Those with large incomes have discovered that they could give more and live on less. For them the simple life is more healthful, more joyful, and more blessed in every way. By responding more generously to the needs of the poor they have experienced the joy of contributing to life, not death. If their monetary resources are not used for killing perhaps then decision-makers will take more seriously their concern to have their tax money channeled into life-sustaining programs rather than into weapons of death. As a single person, Cornelia Lehn of Newton, Kansas, is among those who has selected this option of giving more in order to reduce her complicity in war.[85]

(4) *Limit your income to a nontaxable level.* Most people choose not to live below the taxable line as this would be taking on a standard of living dictated by

government. Others, again, would rather live in "poverty" than break tax laws. For them it is an opportunity to begin living more simply, withdrawing further from consumerism and the war economy. (As one person observed, "Being a tax resister is like being poor—it's a good thing but so inconvenient!") Those who adopt this low-income style of life to avoid tax liability usually seek part-time work, short-term jobs, or limited self-employment. Such a lifestyle represents a sacrificial position financially. However, it is a significant form of witness and is "safe" within the limits of law (not civil disobedience, but accommodation to the law). Eldon and Helen Bargen of Elkhart, Indiana, have been practicing this strategy of war tax protest.

One of the attractive aspects of this strategy is that it permits one to work for an organization or employer who ordinarily cooperates with the IRS by withholding the tax supposedly due from the employee. The form may be signed by any employee who did not have tax liability for the previous year and expects to incur none in the current year. Although it must be signed anew in each calendar year, the form permits the employer to pay the full salary or wage without withholding taxes. Whether this method of tax resistance is for you or not, it certainly keeps money out of military hands!

The W-4E option, while no longer in general use, enables individuals to challenge effectively the vast power being brought to bear by governments on the lives of human beings. As *The Peacemaker* put it:

> One person, by changing himself in accordance with what he deeply believes, begins, at least in a small way, to change the world. Although great social changes are not

59

likely to come about from the effort of a single individual, no significant change can be made without the effort of each of us.[86]

Persons involved in intentional communities are discovering this to be a very satisfying, corporate way of challenging private ownership and accumulated wealth while maintaining a spirit of togetherness and community solidarity. Reba Place Fellowship in Evanston, Illinois, and the Fairview House in Wichita, Kansas, operate as "religious associations" under IRS Code Number 501-D.

(5) Claim additional dependents to eliminate withholding. This is achieved by refiling the W-4 form so that less or no tax is withheld by the employer. (Note: If one claims no tax liability for the previous year, one can also file a W-4 form to eliminate all withholding. Simply enter the word "Exempt" on Line 3.)

Because of the need to be known as persons of integrity the "W-4 resistance" strategy is not always acceptable to Christians. Also persons using this method are more vulnerable for prosecution than with most other methods. However, a change in the law in 1972 now permits people to claim extra exemptions without claiming false numbers of dependents. It is also possible to claim allowances by estimating itemized deductions in advance. Ivan and Rachel Friesen of Swift Current, Sasketchewan, engaged in W-4 refusal during 1972-1973. Finally the taxes which they had consistently refused to pay were confiscated from Rachel's paycheck by the IRS in 1976.[87]

If the tax system of the United States Government is truly based on voluntary compliance, it would be helpful if the Government would be more responsive to how peacemakers feel about the confiscation of citizens' earnings against their moral convictions.

(6) Claim a war tax credit (deduction) or a "refund of taxes illegally, erroneously, or excessively collected."

It may be a surprise to some that there is such a legal channel for recovering money which is intended for the Pentagon. There are two methods and both are very useful to those who are caught in the tax withholding system by virtue of their employment.

(a) One approach is to claim a "war crimes deduction" on "Schedule A—Itemized Deductions" of Form 1040 to bring the taxable income to a desired level. This method has been used successfully by Dr. and Mrs. Joseph Eigner of St. Louis, Missouri,[88] and James R. Klassen of Goessel, Kansas. It relies on a claim that one is not obligated to pay for war or for war crimes which may be based upon the First Amendment right to refuse dollar-participation in war for conscience' sake and/or the Nuremburg Principles which assert that "individual human beings are responsible for their acts." This method makes the allowances of the W-4 claim consistent and shows that the W-4 form is not fradulent.

(b) Another approach is to file for a refund using IRS Form 843. This claim form entitles citizens to call for a "refund of taxes illegally, erroneously, or excessively collected." It is available to any citizen who wishes to recover paid taxes. Claims may be filed within three years from the date of payment. In the 1960s noted folk singer-pacifist Joan Baez made this claim with the IRS, requesting that 60 percent of her withheld tax be returned.[89] Taxpayers Against War feel this strategy has several advantages: it is within the law, the government does not get additional money in penalties to purchase more weapons, and it allows the person who has taxes withheld (and therefore can't refuse payment) to protest in a significant way without experiencing a sort of constant niggling harassment that is dehumanizing and which finally is in direct opposition to the spirit of the witness.

Whether or not these two closely related methods achieve the goal of diverting money from the military they do provide us with another means of making a Christian witness to our society about the proper use of tax monies. We believe the effort is not wasted.

(7) Pay taxes under protest. Persons who are not prepared to refuse payment on a portion or all of their income taxes can certainly exercise the freedom to include a letter along with their payment. These cards and letters should be directed to the Internal Revenue Service with copies also going to congresspersons, the secretary of Tax Legislation, and the president. By paying under protest one is able to represent his views to the state without incurring the penalties that accompany the nonpayment of taxes. During the 1960s the Women's International League for Peace and Freedom made available a blue sticker which read: "That part of this income tax which is levied for preparation for war is paid only under protest." Since 1977 the National Council of the World Peace Tax Fund Act has circulated cards and encouraged citizens to engage in a write-in campaign to their representatives. Through this effort they expect to facilitate a growing Christian witness to government on the stewardship of money—to promote better ways of living instead of better ways of killing.

(8) Decline to pay or to cooperate with IRS attempts to collect taxes. This strategy necessitates earning a tax-

able income outside of the withholding system. There are types of work which do not come under the withholding rule of the IRS. Although exempt from withholding, such jobs are not exempt from tax, so people in these jobs have prime opportunity to refuse to pay. Ammon Hennacy of Utah is an example of a person who felt himself to be violated by the introduction of the withholding system. To preserve a small part of his morality, he quit his job and worked as a transient for eleven years, rather than pay taxes for war.[90] John Howard Yoder believes that at times,

> . . . the most effective way to take responsibility is to refuse to collaborate. . . . This refusal is not a withdrawal from society. It is rather a negative intervention within the process of social change, a refusal to use unworthy means even for what seems to be a worthy end.[91]

Nonpayment involves civil disobedience—refusing to obey a government order. This is an area of some controversy and involves risks. The refusal of conscientious objectors to become a part of the military during World War I was a significant factor in the ultimate development of the alternative service programs of World War II. It is this historical precedent which gives credence to these present-day alternatives to war taxes. Some tax refusers are convinced that nothing short of the most intense pressure will ever bring about change in anything as unyielding as the military establishment.

(9) File a 1040 Form but pay taxes selectively. Some persons calculate the percentage of the federal budget which is used for military purposes (i.e., 40 to 70 percent or a more precise figure) and then deduct that amount from their payment. Many persons choose voluntarily to

contribute the withheld portion to charities, peace organizations or UNICEF as a positive expression of their convictions. This method is useful when part of one's tax has been withheld from one's salary, and the IRS is claiming more, or if one is self-employed and owes IRS money. Obviously, self-employed persons not subject to withholding may do this more readily than those employed by a firm. The objection to this strategy is that the same proportion of what one does pay will still go for war preparations. Still, there is a world of difference between handing money over to the IRS without question and making them come seize it.

Refusal to pay these taxes subjects one to possible criminal prosecution by the government. Experiences vary but generally it can be stated that the government is more interested in collecting taxes than pressing criminal charges.[92] True, those who actively resist war taxes will discover that eventually the money can be taken by the IRS and the military, yet not without sparking some public interest and provoking numerous forums in which to voice one's concern. This has been the experience of Stan and Janet Reedy of Elkhart, Indiana, after deciding not to pay voluntarily 60 percent of their income tax. They are prepared to stop redirecting their tax money when the government reorders its priorities in favor of life over death. Jack Cady of Port Townsend, Washington, has also made his witness in a similar manner.[93]

(10) *Notify your employer of your conscientious objector stance on war taxes and request that such taxes not be withheld.* The employer will usually claim there is nothing he can do. (This was true for Cornelia Lehn, cited earlier.) However, there is always some value in having raised the issue. In an effort to challenge "the

64

threshold of legality" the American Friends Service Committee has worked energetically to protect and to promote the religious freedom of its employees. Louis W. Schneider stated:

> . . . As an organization we have always paid our taxes, but we are vehemently opposed to being compelled to act as tax collector against the conscience of employees. We believe that the employee has the right to confront the government directly on this issue and we should not be made to play the role of middleman.[94]

A. J. Muste (1885-1967) observed that if a tax refuser

> has a bank account or is earning wages or salary, the government can quite readily collect the money. At that point, the question arises whether temporary refusal to pay is more than a gesture, which gives one some inner satisfaction but achieves no social purpose, especially since "tax refusal" on this level—or perhaps on any—may have little or no actual economic effect. To this question one may answer that it is still much better *especially in a society which is geared to inducing conformity and making protest difficult,* to register some protest which makes one's neighbors, and also the public . . . pause and think, than it is to let the hideous business of collecting billions for nuclear war purposes go on smoothly without a voice being raised against it at the crucial moment when payment is demanded.[95]

(11) File a blank return. Using this strategy, people submit either a 1040 or 1040A form with their name and address at the top and their signature at the bottom, but nothing more. An attached letter explains that they consider themselves protected by the Fifth Amendment, as providing financial information could be evidence of

complicity in war crimes. The IRS may try to set a figure on the tax owed and then attempt to collect it.

(12) Refuse to file. There are those, like A. J. Muste of New York, who choose not to file a report at all. However uncompromising his stand appeared to be, it was observed that "when a man as respected as A. J. refuses to pay taxes, it's like Jeremiah walking down the street naked. People stop, look, and listen."[96] Muste's decision to pay *no* income tax was based on the fact that a huge percentage of whatever one pays must be thought of as going for war purposes. Willful failure to file a return is punishable by up to a year in prison and a $10,000 fine, plus costs of prosecution. For eleven years beginning in 1944, Walter Gormly of Mount Vernon, Iowa, reported his income but did not pay. He also then refused to file, because the IRS assessed penalties for not filing as a result of his refusal to sign the statement swearing to the return's accuracy.[97]

There are other options in addition to the twelve outlined above. Consult the handbooks for more information. To build a sense of community on the war tax issue it has been proposed that as many persons as possible withhold ten to twenty dollars of the federal income tax. An accompanying note would explain that this small token is a natural consequence the military must suffer for having such an oversized budget. It would also explain how this money would be used to meet human needs. Based on people's experience with the phone tax this approach would be unlikely to result in any legal proceedings. However, this shared experience would communicate a valid concern which could have empowering effects for the participants. This action would be symbolic, of course. Estimates of *real* dollars going to war purposes vary between 40 and 55 percent of the Congressionally controllable federal budget.[98]

In Solitary Witness

As we noted in the life of Henry David Thoreau, the individual's witness is not to be disparaged. Franz Jägerstätter, a relatively untutored farmer living in a remote village of Austria during Adolf Hitler's time of political power, wrestled with basic vocational questions. On the basis of his New Testament readings he experienced conflict in trying to satisfy simultaneously the demands of the community of God and the Nazi folk community. Definitely preferring to preserve his rights granted under the kingdom of God, Jägerstätter deliberately refused military service in Hitler's army. For this act of dissent he was imprisoned and finally beheaded on August 9, 1943.

The account of this modern saint is the more remarkable because he was able to reach this decision without the support of family, friends, or his own religious community. He rejected the plea from each of them to bend and therefore survive. Inspired by the Scriptures and the Holy Spirit this heroic peasant went knowingly to his death. Determined to be loyal to God he confronted his Caesar with a good conscience. By meditation and prayer God led this man, who tested in life what he heard in his conscience, along a difficult but good path.

In retrospect we see this costly discipleship of Jesus as being good for others as well as for Jägerstätter himself. Faint-hearted obedience to Hitler could never have compensated him for the satisfaction of doing the will of the Almighty.[99] Jägerstätter's experience underscores the fact that "we must learn to live with social alienation

67

since it is part of the price for recalling one another to the demands of the (Christian) covenant."[100] The individual conscience against the demonic powers. There is no other way.

Refusing the Old Powers

Not all of us are able to make our Christian witness alone as Franz Jägerstätter did. Although it is often said that "God and I are a majority" most of us need the support of persons who care. A prophet needs a fellowship base; a dissenter needs a caring community. Most of us need to band together for courage and action. Perhaps Christopher Fry caught the feeling in the character Tim Meadows:

> Dark and cold we may be, but this
> Is no winter now. The frozen misery
> Of centuries breaks, cracks, begins to move,
> The thunder is the thunder of the foes,
> The thaw, the flood, the upstart Spring.
> Thank God our time is now when wrong
> Comes up to face us everywhere,
> Never to leave us till we take
> The longest stride of soul men ever took.
> Affairs are now soul size.
> The enterprise
> Is exploration into God.
> Where are you going? It takes
> So many thousand years to wake,
> But will you wake for pity's sake,
> Pete's sake, Dave or one of you,
> Wake up, will you? . . .[101]

The need to get our Christian faith off the level of talk and writing and onto the level of action is imperative.

But the difficulty of achieving this objective is clarified for us by Doug Hostetter:

> For 400 years we Mennonites have had a theology of complete peace and noncooperation in war. But the fact is we have been at war with the Vietnamese. We have paid our taxes which have bought the bombs that have killed the people. We have cooperated with Selective Service even when we have not gone into the military. We have said if there is conflict between Christ and the government, we choose Christ. But in the last fifty years we have never felt we had to make a decision against the government. [102]

That is a serious indictment of our failure to practice the gospel we hear and preach. Unless Christians recognize the interrelatedness of money and the military we will discover to our dismay that the graves of our dead enemies will have been dug with the coins engraved, "In God We Trust." What blasphemy! Will we continue indefinitely to sin against God with "our" property? Will the "authorities" forever intimidate us in our witness for Christ? Will there always be a contradiction in our lives—a profession of allegiance to the Prince of Peace and a denial of it in our tax payments for war?

Let us hope that the values on which we base our lives will make the paying of war taxes an obvious impossibility. Could the Holy Spirit prevent our hands from writing checks that go for war and motivate us to write more checks for peace and justice? Could we tell the tax collector in action clear enough for all the world to see that we have committed ourselves to LIFE? The sixteenth-century Anabaptists have given us a model to emulate.

They simply refused the old powers and institutions the authority which they were claiming over people. They began to live as though the kingdom of God, whose final arrival they anticipated, had already fully come. They said in their day "the war is over," and commenced to live in peace.[103]

There is further precedent for this model in the testimony and ethical worship of the first-century church. With the fear of the Lord before their eyes they asserted their deep commitment to love: "When anyone is united to Christ, there is a new world; the old order has gone, and a new order has already begun" (2 Corinthians 5:17, NEB). Is it any wonder, then, that John Woolman recognized "the advantage of living in the real substance of religion, where practice doth harmonize with principle"?[104]

Will we who live in the twentieth century also issue the call to living and acting as though the old institutions no longer tyranize? Who will perform a death-defying act? The choice is up to us. Because her church believes in the way of peace, Cornelia Lehn wants all to stand up in horror and refuse to help the government to make war, declaring, "We will not give you our sons and daughters and we will not give you our money to kill others."[105] "Dealing with a problem of this proportion will be costly," John Drescher has warned.

It may demand a different lifestyle, the loss of property and institutions. We can be assured, however, that the way of obedience, even though it leads through the wilderness and death, is the way of Christ. Out of death we believe there is always a resurrection. And how our world needs resurrection life![106]

In the words of Melvin Schmidt, the prophetic tax refuser

measures his action only in terms of God's ultimate purpose for the world and the radical demands of Christ. An analogous situation is the case of the pacifist who is charged by his compatriots with not being a "good patriot" because of his refusal to bear arms. The pacifist rejects the criterion of the other citizens and sees himself as being a "good patriot" for entirely different, and higher, reasons. Likewise, prophetic tax refusal is not a denial of responsibility for the social situation, but acceptance of it in a personal encounter with evil.[107]

One Act of Dedication

The struggles of Jesus are ours too. Like Him, it is our task to unmask the subtle idolatries. Like Him too, we take our cues from history, but our call from beyond history. Interestingly enough, Jesus found a way of meeting at once the claims of Caesar and those of God. He was not torn between the two. The way He put it together, there is only one act of dedication which fulfills the demand of Caesar and the demand of God. That act is obedience to God even to the point of death. (See Philippians 2:8).

Anyone who embarks on such a course must be prepared for the fiery furnace—or the cross. Actually, Jesus' death on the cross is the model of what it means to render to Caesar what is Caesar's and to God what is God's. Apparently, Jesus did not think that His aggressive confrontation with the Jewish authorities violated the law of love. Instead it suggested that love can and should take certain forms of resistance. Because of conflicting values, Caesar eventually demanded of Jesus His life, and Jesus paid it. In doing this His life was simultaneously in a much profounder sense given to God. As Marlin Jeschke points out, Jesus' life and death is finally the best interpretation and answer to the question about paying taxes.

> . . . Caesar may rob us of our money as he may rob us of our life. But these, both money and life, are really God's. With Jesus we must start with the act of devoting them to the kingdom. This then exposes Caesar as the invader that he is, whose taxation of people may actually be an act of plunder.
>
> The problem for many people whose conscience bothers them about paying taxes is that they have somehow accepted the state system too positively. They have forgotten the fallenness and rapaciousness of Caesar. And they have perhaps also forgotten that the discipled community is a radical alternative.[108]

Strange as it seems, good news is seldom perceived as such. Therefore, Jesus' disciples must be prepared for rejection and persecution.

Although Jesus never became a Zealot (a militant revolutionary) he was condemned to death as a Zealot by the Romans. This insight tells us that we must be willing to be understood by others in a less favorable, more revolutionary way than we understand ourselves. In our opposition to war taxes, Willard Swartley believes that

> we must accept the liability that political forces will brand both our resistance and nonresistance as revolutionary. But it might just well be that this discrepancy between their perception and our self-understanding is the critical test of our faithfulness to the ethic of Jesus.[109]

In the Nuclear Age the institutions of war are not only

murderous of persons but of human existence itself. To help them thrive by means of one's life, whether that life be spent in military service or in the payment of heavy war taxes, is to sow death across mankind's future. Therefore, to be freed from the clutches of a war economy might be the most appropriate act of repentance for us to do. But it could be a costly discipleship. It will happen only when we join the Lamb's War—when we commit ourselves to the task of incarnating the Jesus lifestyle of servanthood. To render to Caesar the things that are Caesar's is to bear in mind always that it was Caesar's cross on which Jesus died so that "the Christian, too, may finally have to render to Caesar a cross rather than a denarius."[110]

... We could succeed in not paying taxes and still miss the kingdom. We could also fail in resisting tax payment and *also* fail to have taken up the life of the kingdom....[111]

Our task then, individually and corporately, is to "render to Caesar the things that are Caesar's," but above all to "give to God what is His, perhaps in conflict with everything else."[112] Martin Buber has assured us that "those who know God dare dread no earthly power."[113]

Claiming God's Ability to Do the Impossible
Not everything that needs to be done on the war tax problem is illegal. But if it is illegal it certainly "is a high crime to break the laws of Jesus Christ in order to yield obedience to earthly rulers."[114] God help us to throw off our timidity, and with courage, joy, and boldness to act more meaningfully. Recognizing the principalities and powers at work in our world, let us, like discriminating

disciples of the past, be selective in the taxes we agree to pay.[115] May God arm our respective communities with such inner strength that we will need no military weapons for defense or for expansion. Fortunately,

> God never fails to offer the strength to deal with the consequences of following His will. This is a fundamental part of His covenant with persons. With God's love, we are truly liberated from the limitations of this world.[116]

> Having no gift of strategy, no arms,
>> No secret weapon and no walled defense,
>>> I shall become a citizen of love,
> That little nation with the blood-stained sod
> Where even the slain have power, the only country
>> That sends forth an ambassador to God.
> Renouncing self and crying out to evil
>> To end its wars, I seek a land that lies
>> All unprotected like a sleeping child.
>>> Nor is my journey reckless and unwise.
> Who doubts that love has an effective weapon
>> May meet with a surprise.[117]

God's amazing love can make possible creative responses to seemingly impossible situations—even the impossible task of resolving the war tax problem. As we trust the Holy Spirit we too will find solutions, some conventional and some unconventional. Seeking first His kingdom, and accepting this problem as a gift of God, we are therefore able to live. Jesus said:

> Happy are those who work for peace;
>> God will call them his children!
> Happy are those who are persecuted because they do what
>> God requires; the Kingdom of heaven belongs to them!
>>> —Matthew 5:9, 10, TEV.

74

NOTES AND REFERENCES

1. Jeanette Rankin, first woman in Congress and the only member of Congress to vote against both World Wars. Quoted by David Wood in "Militarism: A $10-A-Week Habit" (122 W. Franklin Ave., Minneapolis, Minn.: Minnesota Clergy & Laity Concerned), p. 1.

2. Staughton Lynd (editor), *Nonviolence in America: A Documentary History* (New York: Bobbs-Merrill, 1966), p. xxxiii.

3. Nat Hentoff (editor), *The Essays of A. J. Muste* (Indianapolis, New York, and Kansas City: The Bobbs-Merrill, 1967), p. 371.

4. Will Durant and Ariel Durant, *The Lessons of History* (3533 W. Pico Blvd., Los Angeles, Calif., 90019: S & S Enterprises, 1968).

5. Donald D. Kaufman, *What Belongs to Caesar?* (Scottdale, Pa.: Herald Press, 1969; 1973 Revised Bibliography), p. 31.

6. Frank H. Epp, "On the topic of the tax," *The Mennonite* (March 7, 1961), p. 151.

7. Donald F. Durnbaugh (editor), *The Brethren in Colonial America* (Elgin, Ill.: The Brethren Press, 1967), pp. 364-5; John C. Wenger, *History of the Mennonites of the Franconia Conference* (Telford, Pa.: Franconia Mennonite Historical Society, 1937), p. 410; and John C. Wenger, *Pacifism and Biblical Nonresistance* (Scottdale, Pa.: Herald Press, 1968), p. 26.

8. Dale W. Brown, "The Bible on Tax Resistance," *Sojourners* (March, 1977), pp. 13-14.

9. John Howard Yoder, "The Things That Are Caesar's" (Part I), *Christian Living* (July, 1960), p. 5; *The Christian Witness to the State* (Newton, Kan.: Faith and Life Press, 1964), p. 75; and *The Politics of Jesus* (Grand Rapids, Mich.: Eerdmans, 1972), pp. 163-214.

10. Robert Friedmann, "Claus Felbinger's Confession of 1560," *Mennonite Quarterly Review*, XXIX (April, 1955), p. 145, and Walter Klaassen, "Mennonites and War Taxes," p. 3 (mimeographed) p. 5 (printed edition, Newton, Kans.: Faith and Life Press, 1978) portions were first presented to the Mennonite War Tax Conference held at Kitchener, Ontario, on November 1, 1975.

11. The quotation is by an unnamed participant in a 1977 consultation on the draft and national service held in Kansas City, Mo. (Bulletin # 4782, Faith and Life Press, North Newton, Kans.: 67117).

12. *The Interpreter's Bible* and numerous other commentaries: Commission on Home Ministries (CCMC) "Resource Packet on Civil Reponsibility," Elkhart, Indiana, Consultation, June 1-4, 1978 (Box 347, Newton, Kans.: 67114, Cost: $1.50)

Brown, Dale W. "Some Possibilities for a Biblical Case for Tax Refusal," *Brethren Life and Thought*, Vol. XIX (Spring, 1974) pp. 101-112.

Cranfield, C. E. B., *A Commentary on Romans 12—13*.

Cullmann, Oscar, *The State in the New Testament*.

Durnbaugh, Donald F. (ed.) *On Earth Peace* (Discussions on War/ Peace Issues Between Friends, Mennonites, Brethren, and European Churches, 1935-75).

Eller, Vernard, *King Jesus' Manual of Arms for the Armless* (War and Peace from Genesis to Revelation).

Fast, Henry A., *Jesus and Human Conflict*.

Kaufman, Donald D., *What Belongs to Caesar?* (esp. chapters II & III).

Keeney, William, "Fighting Like Heaven"

Kehler, Larry, *The Rule of the Lamb*.

Kennard, J. Spencer, Jr., *Render to God*.

Kraybill, Donald B., *Our Star-Spangled Faith* (esp. chapter 10) and *The Upside-Down Kingdom*.

Kuenning, Larry, *Exiles in Babylon*.

Lasserre, Jean, *War and the Gospel*.

Macgregor, G. H. C., *The New Testament Basis of Pacifism* (Revised Edition).

Rutenber, Culbert G., *The Dagger and the Cross*.

Swartley, Willard, "The Christian and Payment of War Taxes" (mimeographed study presented to the Mennonite War Tax Conference held at Kitchener, Ontario, on November 1, 1975).

Trocmé, André, *Jesus and the Nonviolent Revolution*.

Yoder, John Howard, *The Christian Witness to the State* and *The Politics of Jesus*.

For additional bibliography see *What Belongs to Caesar?*, pp. 104-122.

13. William Stringfellow, *An Ethic for Christians and Other Aliens in a Strange Land* (Waco, Texas: Word Books, 1973), pp. 72-73.

14. The writer of Psalm 51 prays: "O Lord God, my deliverer, save me from bloodshed [or blood guiltiness], and I will sing the praises of thy justice" (verse 14, NEB). Also Isaiah (1:15b) reflects on God's attitude toward bloodshed: "Even though you make many prayers, I will not listen: your hands are full of blood."

15. John E. Steen, "Death and Taxes" leaflet (204½ W. Third St., Santa Ana, Calif.: Orange Country Peace and Human Rights Center, 1969).

16. Richard K. MacMaster, *Christian Obedience in Revolutionary Times: The Peace Churches and the American Revolution* (Akron,

Pa.: Mennonite Central Committee, Peace Section, 1976), p. 16 and John L. Ruth,'*Twas Seeding Time: A Mennonite View of the American Revolution* (Scottdale, Pa.: Herald Press, 1976), pp. 58-59.

17. John L. Ruth, *Ibid.*, p. 71.

18. *Ibid.*, p. 163.

19. Wilhelm Mensching, *Conscience* (Wallingford, Pa.: Pendle Hill Pamphlets by Sowers Printing Company, Lebanon, Pa., August, 1961), p. 15.

20. John M. Drescher, "Taxes for War" (an editorial), *Gospel Herald* (June 27, 1972), p. 545.

21. Kenneth Cragg in the introduction to M. Kamel Hussein's *City of Wrong: A Friday in Jerusalem* (Amsterdam, The Netherlands: N. V. Djambatan, 1959), p. xiv.

22. M. Kamel Hussein, *City of Wrong, op. cit.*, p. 68.

23. *Ibid.*, pp. 123-4.

24. Karl Menninger, *Whatever Became of Sin?* (New York: Hawthorne Books, Inc., 1973), p. 99.

25. For a more objective account covering a period of four centuries see the author's mimeographed article, "A Chronology of Wars Reflecting the 'Anabaptist' Response to War Taxes," first presented to the Mennonite War Tax Conference, Kitchener, Ontario, Canada, Oct. 30 to Nov. 1, 1975 (28 pages including footnotes).

26. Harold S. Bender, "Taxation," *Mennonite Encyclopedia*, Vol. IV (Scottdale, Pa.: Mennonite Publishing House, 1959), p. 688. See also Peter Brock, *Pacifism in Europe to 1914* (Princeton, N.J.: Princeton Unviersity Press), pp. 236-9, 243; Walter Klaassen, "Mennonites and War Taxes," *op. cit.*, pp. 10-11. (mimeographed), pp 12-13 (printed edition).

27. Robert Friedmann, "Claus Felbinger's Confession of 1560," *op. cit.*, p. 147, and Walter Klaassen, *Anabaptism: Neither Catholic nor Protestant* (Waterloo, Ont.: Conrad Press, 1973), p. 56.

28. Ernest R. Bomley, "The Case for Tax Refusal," *Fellowship* (November, 1974), p. 172.

29. Franklin Zahn (compiler), "Historical Notes on Conscience vs. War Taxes," p. 1.

30. Guy F. Hershberger, *Nonresistance and the State* (Scottdale, Pa.: Mennonite Publishing House, 1937), p. 33. For a comprehensive account of the Quaker peace testimony see Peter Brock, *Pioneers of the Peaceable Kingdom* (Princeton, N.J.: Princeton University Press, 1968), 382 pages.

31. Isaac Sharpless, *A Quaker Experiment in Government* quoted in Melvin D. Schmidt, "Tax Refusal as Conscientious Objection to

War," *Mennonite Quarterly Review* Vol. XLIII (July, 1969), p. 234.

32. Janet Whitney (ed.), *The Journal of John Woolman* (Chicago, Ill.: Henry Regnery Company, 1950), pp. 66, 68.

33. Margaret E. Hirst, *The Quakers in Peace and War* (New York: George H. Doran Company, 1923), pp. 344-349, 367-382; and Donald F. Durnbaugh (editor), *The Brethren in Colonial America, op. cit.,* pp. 145-6.

34. Robert Calvert (compiler and editor), *Ain't Gonna Pay for War No More*, 2nd Edition (New York: War Tax Resistance, 1972), p. 37. And Peter Brock, *Pacifism in the United States: From the Colonial Era to First World War* (Princeton, N.J.: Princeton University Press, 1968), pp. 150-2. The official query of the Society of Friends periodically read in its Meetings was, "Are you faithful in maintaining our Christian testimony against all war as inconsistent with the precepts and spirit of the gospel?"

35. Donald F. Durnbaugh, *op. cit.,* p. 146.

36. John L. Ruth, *op. cit.,* pp. 64, 81-92; 162-195; and Richard K. MacMaster, *op. cit.,* p. 18. See also J. S. Hartzler and Daniel Kauffman, *Mennonite Church History* (Scottdale, Pa.: Mennonite Book and Tract Society, 1905), p. 165; "Christian Funk and the Schism Among the Mennonites. His Stand for Loyalty," *The Mennonite* (July 15, 1920), pp. 1-3; Guy F. Hershberger, *War, Peace, and Nonresistance* (Scottdale, Pa.: Herald Press, 1946), pp. 94-5; Millard Lind, *Answer to War* (Scottdale, Pa.: Herald Press, 1952), pp. 63-4; and William Warren Sweet, *The Story of Religion in America* (New York: Harper and Brothers, 1930, 1950), p. 187. Authors Ruth and Lind believe that Mennonites agonized over both the conflicting demands of two Caesars and the legitimacy of war tax payments.

37. Quoted by Donald F. Durnbaugh, *The Brethren in Colonial America, op. cit.,* pp. 364-5; and Wilbur Bender, *Nonresistance in Colonial Pennsylvania* (Scottdale, Pa.: Mennonite Publishing House, 1934), p. 18.

38. Peter M. Friesen, *The Mennonite Brotherhood in Russia* (1789-1910) Translated from the German. (Fresno, Calif.: Board of Christian Literature, G.C. of Mennonite Brethren Churches, 1978), pp 50, 87ff. Frank H. Epp, *Mennonites in Canada, 1786-1920; The History of a Separate People* (Toronto: Macmillan of Canada, 1974), p. 48; H. Penner, "West Prussian Mennonites Through Four Centuries," *Mennonite Quarterly Review*, XXIII (1949), pp. 242-3; John B. Toews, "The Origins and Activities of the Mennonite 'Selbstschutz' in the Ukraine" (1918-1919), *Mennonite Quarterly Review*, XLVI (January, 1972), p. 10; and Walter Klaassen, "Mennonites and War Taxes," *op. cit.,* p. 16. (mimeographed), p. 19 (printed edition).

39. Harold S. Bender, "Kleine Gemeinde," *Mennonite Encyclopedia*, Vol. III, p. 196; Paul Toews (editor), *Pilgrims and Strangers* (Essays in Mennonite Brethren History), (4824 E. Butler, Fresno, Calif. 93727: Center for Mennonite Brethren Studies, MBBS, 1977), pp. 58 and 62; John A. Toews, *A History of the Mennonite Brethren Church* (Fresno, Calif.: Board of Christian Literature, 1975), pp. 26-29; Mary Lou Cummings (editor), *Full Circle* (Newton, Kans.: Faith and Life Press, 1978), pp. 192 and 194.

40. Staughton Lynd (editor), *op. cit.*, pp. 41-2.

41. Lillian Schlissel (editor), *Conscience in America* (New York: E. P. Dutton & Co., Inc., 1968), p. 77.

42. Henry David Thoreau, *Walden* and *On the Duty of Civil Disobedience* (New York: Collier Books, 1962), esp. pp. 236-55; see also Ammon Hennacy, *The One-Man Revolution in America* (Salt Lake City, Utah: Ammon Hennacy Publications, 1970), pp. 68-88 and James Daugherty (editor), *Henry David Thoreau: A Man for Our Time* (New York: Viking Press, 1967).

43. Larry Gara, *War Resistance in Historical Perspective* (Wallingford, Pa.: Pendle Hill Pamphlets #171,1970), p.11; H.A. De Boer, *The Bridge Is Love* (London: Marshall, Morgan and Scott, 1957), p. 112.

44. Leo Tolstoy. *Writings on Civil Disobedience and Non-Violence* (New York: The New American Library, Inc., 1967), p. 23; Arthur and Lila Weinberg (ed.), *Instead of Violence* (Boston, Mass.: Beacon Press, 1963), p. 329.

45. Carl D. Soule, Review of *Conscientious Objection in the Civil War*, by Edward Needles Wright, *The Reporter for Conscience' Sake*, XIX (June, 1962), p. 2.

46. Guy F. Hershberger, *War, Peace, and Nonresistance*, *op. cit.*, p. 99; Peter Brock, *Pacifism in the United States*, *op. cit.*, p. 763.

47. *The Laws of the State of Kansas* passed at the Fourteenth Annual Session of the Legislature, commenced at the State Capital on Tuesday, Jan. 13, 1874 (Topeka, Kans.: State Printing Works, 1874), p. 134; C. Henry Smith, *Christian Peace: Four Hundred Years of Mennonite Peace Principles and Practice* (Peace Committee of the General Conference of the Mennonite Church of North America, 1938), p. 21; C. Henry Smith, *The Coming of the Russian Mennonites: An Episode in the Settling of the Last Frontier*, 1874-1884, (Berne, Ind.: Mennonite Book Concern, 1927), p. 266; David C. Wedel, *The Story of Alexanderwohl, 1874-1974* (Goessel, Kans.: Goessel Centennial Committee, 1974), p. 27.

48. Gene Sharp, *The Politics of Nonviolent Action* (Boston, Mass.: Porter Sargent Publishing, 1973), p. 242.

49. Peter Brock, *Pacifism in Europe to 1914*, *op. cit.*, p. 439, C. J.

79

Dyck, *An Introduction to Mennonite History* (Scottdale, Pa.: Herald Press, 1967), pp. 140-1; and esp. John B. Toews, *op. cit.*, pp. 15-40.

50. Sanford Calvin Yoder, *For Conscience Sake: A Study of Mennonite Migrations Resulting from the World War*, (Scottdale, Pa.: Herald Press, 1945), p. 47.

51. Keith L. Sprunger, James C. Juhnke, and John D. Waltner, *Voices Against War: A Guide to the Schowalter Oral History Collection on World War I Conscientious Objection*, (North Newton, Kans.: Bethel College, 1973), page 2 from the Introductory Forward by James Juhnke. See also Ray H. Abrams, *Preachers present Arms* (Scottdale, Pa,: Herald Press, 1933, 1969), pp. 77-92, 188.

52. Margaret Entz, "War Bond Drives and the Kansas Mennonite Response,"*Mennonite Life* (September, 1975), p. 9. This six-page article is a comprehensive treatment of the Liberty Loan campaigns during World War I and of their impact on Mennonite life. It won the Bethel College Mennonite Contributions contest in 1975.

53. James C. Juhnke, "John Schrag Espionage Case," *Mennonite Life* (July, 1967), pp. 121-2. Charles Gordon's testimony concerning the persecution of John Schrag appears on pages 20-21 of *Mennonite Life* (September, 1975). Additional information is to be found in James C. Juhnke's *A People of Two Kingdoms: The Political Acculturation of the Kansas Mennonites* (North Newton, Kans.: Faith and Life Press, 1975), p. 104, and in Donald E. Durnbaugh's *The Believers' Church* (New York: The Macmillan Company, 1968), p. 258.

54. Elizabeth Hershberger Bauman, *Coals of Fire* (Scottdale, Pa.: Herald Press, 1954), p. 37.

55. John A. Hostetler, *op. cit.*, pp. 130 and 197; C. Henry Smith, *The Coming of the Russian Mennonites*, *op. cit.*, pp. 292-3, 276-82; Cornelius J. Dyck, *op. cit.*, pp. 236-7 (section on "The Hutterites"); and Ray H. Abrams, *op. cit.*, p. 188.

56. James Russell Lowell (1819-1891) in his poem, "The Present Crisis." Included in *The Brethren Hymnal* (Elgin, Ill.: Brethren Publishing House, 1951), Hymn 569.

57. Rufus D. Bowman, *The Church of the Brethren and War* (Elgin, Ill.: Brethren Press, 1944), pp. 238 ff; Dale W. Brown, *Brethren and Pacifism* (Elgin, Ill.: Brethren Press, 1970), p. 47.

58. Austin Regier, "Christianity and Conscription as Viewed by a Non-Registrant," *The Mennonite* (November 30, 1948), pp. 13-15, and "The Faith of a Convict," *The Mennonite* (Feb. 15, 1949) pp. 8-10.

59. Quoted in a War Resisters League leaflet; Nat Hentoff, *Peace Agitator: The Story of A. J. Muste* (New York: The Macmillan Company, 1963), esp. pp. 125-9; editorial on "A. J. Muste," *Fellowship* (March, 1967), p. 3.

60. Robert Calvert, *op. cit.*, p. xiii; Lillian Schlissel, *op cit.*, pp 398 ff; *Handbook on Nonpayment of War Taxes* (Cincinnati, Ohio: Peacemaker Movement, 1963, 1966, 1967, 1968, 1971), 50 pages. Current address of *The Peacemaker* Magazine is: Box 4793, Arcata, Calif. 95521.

61. Marion Bromley, "No Reason to Fear," *Friends Journal* (February 15, 1976), pp. 106-107.

62. Wendy Schwartz, "Tax Resistance and WRL," *WRL News* (July-August 1974), pp. 5-6.

63. "They Would Not Fight" flyer and a personal letter from Bob Seeley of CCCO dated April 14, 1978, 2 pages. The address of CCCO is: 2016 Walnut Street, Philadelphia, Pa. 19103.

64. Thomas C. Cornell and James H. Forest (editors), *A Penny a Copy: Readings from the Catholic Worker* (New York: The Macmillan Co., 1968), pp. 52-3.

65. *Sojourners* (March, 1977), p. 23; Jim Forest and Wes Michaelson, "Encountering Dorothy Day," *Sojourners* (Dec., 1976), pp. 12-19; Joan Thomas, *The Years of Grief and Laughter* (Phoenix, Arizona. Hennacy Press, 1974), 342 pages.

66. "A Plea for the Support of the War Tax Objector" (October, 1971), 7 pages; Bernard Survil, "War: Individual Witness or Corporate Response," p. 2.

67 *The Catholic Worker* (October-November, 1977), p. 5. Mailing address is: 36 East First St., New York, NY 10003. See special issue on "The Burden of the Berrigans," *Holy Cross Quarterly*, Vol. 4, No. 1, (January, 1971), 80 pages.

68. Delton Franz, "Military Related Income Taxes," *The Washington Memo*, Vol. X, No. 2 (March-April, 1978), pp. 1-3.

69. The following is only a partial list of war tax statements:
"A Call to Action" by members of the Mennonite and Brethren in Christ Church of North America (Minneapolis, Nov. 21, 1970);
"A Statement of the Church of the Brethren on War" (1451 Dundee Avenue, Elgin, Ill.: The Brethren Press), four pages; also "Obedience to God and Civil Disobedience," four pages.
"Covenant-Statement of War Tax Workshop Participants," Western District Conference Seminar, North Newton, Kans. (Feb. 27, 1971).
"The Way of Peace," A Christian Declaration Adopted by the General Conference Mennonite Church, at Fresno, Calif., August 19, 1971 (Newton, Kans.: Faith and Life Press, 1972), 24 pages.
"Statement Concerning the World Peace Tax Fund" adopted by the Bethel College Mennonite Church, North Newton, Kans.: on June 1, 1975 (*God and Caesar* newsletter, June, 1975, p. 5).
"General Conference War Tax Resolution #33" adopted at St.

Catharines, Ontario, during August 1974 (*God and Caesar* newsletter, January 1975, p. 2).

"A Position Paper on War Taxes" prepared by a task force of the Bethel College Mennonite Church, North Newton, Kans. 67117 (April 3, 1977), 9 pages.

"Waubee Peace Pledge I & II," prepared by participants of a war tax retreat held at Camp Mack, Ind. (November 4-6, 1977).

70. *The Way of Peace, op. cit.*, p. 18; J. Howard Kauffman and Leland Harder, *Anabaptists Four Centuries Later* (Scottdale, Pa. and Kitchener, Ont.: Herald Press, 1975), p. 134.

71. Address: *God and Caesar*, Box 347, Newton, Kans. 67114.

72. "Tax Resistance Group in Japan Gains Support," *The Mennonite* (February 18, 1975), p. 103. "Cites War Tax Resistance in Japan," *Mennonite Weekly Review* (August 31, 1978) p. 6; Michio Ohno, "A Short Study on War Tax Resistance in Japan" (mimeographed article). Address is: Conscientious Objection to Military Tax (COMIT), 2-35-18 Asahigaoka, Hino City, Tokyo 191, Japan. They publish *The Plowshare* with a one-page English summary (overseas subscription, $4).

73. Ruth C. Stoltzfus, "War Tax Research Report: Challenging Withholding Law on First Amendment Grounds," a special study prepared for CHM, General Conference Mennonite Church, Newton, Kans., August, 1975, consisting of 16 pages.

74. J. R. Burkholder, "Radical Pacifism Challenges the Mennonite Church," (paper prepared for the Mennonite Theological Study Group, January 1960), p. 2.

75. Estimated in Fiscal 1977 budget by War Resisters' League, 339 Lafayette St., New York, N.Y. 10012. Canadian readers who may want to trace Canada's development as a manufacturer and merchandiser of war materials, should consult Ernie Regehr's *Making A Killing* (Toronto, Canada: McClelland and Stewart Limited, 1975), 135 pages.

76. For supplementary information see Kaufman, *What Belongs to Caesar? op. cit.*, pp. 64-70; Stuart Chase, *Where's the Money Coming From?* (New York: The Twentieth Century Fund, 1943), 179 pages.

77. *Congressional Record* (February 23, 1966). See also *Churches and Phone Tax Resistance* (122 West Franklin Ave., Minneapolis, Minn.: Minnesota Clergy and Laymen Concerned, 1970).

78. *Ibid;* Diogenes, *The April Game: Secrets of an Internal Revenue Agent* (Chicago, Ill.: Playboy Press, 1973), pp. 52 ff; Lillian Doris (ed), *The American Way in Taxation: Internal Revenue, 1862-1963* (Englewood Cliffs, N.J.: Prentice-Hall, Inc. 1963), 301 pages.

79. Excerpt from the MCC Peace Section, *Washington Memo* (Nov.-Dec., 1973), p. 6.

80. Phil M. Shenk, "World Peace Tax Fund," *The Mennonite* (December 13, 1977), p. 735. (Current address for WPTF's National Office is 2111 Florida Ave., N.W., Washington, D.C. 20008.

81. Telephone tax protest card circulated by Minnesota Clergy and Laity Concerned.

82. Personal conversation on April 21, 1978.

83. Levi O. Keidel, "The Mennonite Credibility Gap," *The Mennonite* (December 23, 1975), p. 731.

84. "Make Gifts Instead of Paying Tax," *Mennonite Weekly Review* (March 22, 1973), p. 6; Linda Schmidt, " 'War Tax' Refusers Persisting," *Mennonite Weekly Review* (August 24, 1978), p. 5.

85. Cornelia Lehn, "My Pilgrimage with War Tax Resistance," *God and Caesar* (June, 1976), p.2.

86. From a leaflet revised in March, 1974.

87. Ivan Friesen, "Letter to the Editor," *God and Caesar* (October, 1975), pp. 4-5.

88. Robert Calvert, *op. cit.*, pp. 58-59; James R. Klassen, "Letters to the IRS," *God and Caesar* (June and July, 1978 issues), pp. 8-10 and pp. 14-15 respectively.

89. Kaufman, *op. cit.*, p. 81; "Baez Files Claim with IRS for Refund of 1965 Tax," *Fellowship Peace Information Edition* (October, 1966), p. 2.

90. Ammon Hennacy, *op. cit.*, p. 334.

91. Quoted by Phil M. Shenk, *op. cit.*, p. 735.

92. Melvin D. Schmidt, *op. cit.*, pp. 240-241.

93. Janet Reedy, "Our Day in Court," *God and Caesar* (June, 1977), pp. 3-6; Jack Cady, "An Open Letter," *Friends Journal* (February 15, 1976) pp. 102-105.

94. John A. Lapp, "Tax Deductions and the Nationalizing of the Churches," *MCC Peace Section Newsletter* (April 15, 1972), p. 1.

95. *Sojourners* (March, 1977), p. 23. Originally printed in the April, 1960, issue of *Liberation* under the title, "Not So Long Ago: My Affair with the Internal Revenue Bureau," pp. 17-19.

96. Nat Hentoff, *op. cit.*, p. 129.

97. Personal letter to author dated April 17, 1978, and a letter which was printed in both *The Peacemaker* (September 2, 1977) and *God and Caesar* (November, 1977), pp. 6-7. Also see Edmund Wilson, *The Cold War and the Income Tax: A Protest* (New York: Farrar, Straus and Company, 1963), pp. 105-107.

98. Dave Wood, *et. al.*, Letter from Minnesota War Tax Resistance and Alternative Fund, 122 W. Franklin, Room 302, Minneapolis, Minn. 55404, dated March 20, 1978.

99. Gordon C. Zahn, Review of *In Solitary Witness: The Life and*

Death of Franz Jägerstätter appearing in *Fellowship* (March, 1965).

100. Kenneth D. Eberhard, *The Alienated Christain: Theology of Alienation* (Philadelphia, Pa.: Pilgrim Press, 1971), p. 133. The book is now available in softbound edition (278 pages) from The Liturgical Press, Collegeville, Minn., 56321.

101. Christopher Fry, *A Sleep of Prisoners* (a play) (New York and London: Oxford University Press, 1951), pp. 47-8.

102. Howard E. Royer, "Portraits of Asia," *Messenger* (February 15, 1971), p. 31. (A people-to-people peace treaty undertaking of the National Student Association by Doug Hostetter in Vietnam, December, 1970.)

103. Walter Klaassen, *Anabaptism: Neither Catholic nor Protestant, op. cit.,* p. 81.

104. Margaret E. Hirst, *op. cit.* p. 347, or P. Mayer, *The Pacifist Conscience* (New York: Holt, Rinehart and Winston, 1966), p. 97.

105. Donald D. Kaufman, "Paying for war while praying for peace: dilemma of individuals and the body," *Sojourners* (March, 1977), p. 17.

106. John M. Drescher, *op. cit.,* p.545.

107. Melvin D. Schmidt, *op. cit.,* p. 245.

108. Marlin Jeschke, "Render to Caesar or to God?" (Revision of a presentation made to the Peace Assembly in Chicago, Illinois, during November 16-18, 1972; revised on March 20, 1973), p. 3.

109. Willard Swartley, "The Christian and Payment of War Taxes" (Mimeographed study presented to the Mennonite War Tax Conference held at Kitchener, Ontario, on November 1, 1975), p. 10.

110. James W. Douglass, *The Non-Violent Cross: A Theology of Revolution and Peace* (London: The Macmillan Company, 1966, 1968), p. 213; see also Charlie Lord, *The Rule of the Sword* (Newton, Kans.: Faith and Life Press, 1978), 68 pages.

111. Marlin Jeschke, *op.cit.,* p. 3.

112. Jean Lasserre, *War and the Gospel* (Scottdale, Pa.: Herald Press, 1962), p. 92. The Apostle Peter in Acts 4:19 and 5:29.

113. Martin Buber, Will Herberg (editor), *The Writings of Martin Buber* (New York: New American Library, 1958), p. 28.

114. Pope Leo XIII quoted by Ammon Hennacy, *The Book of Ammon* (P.O. Box 655, Salt Lake City, Utah, 1965), p. 298.

115. Arthur G. Gish, *The New Left and Christian Radicalism* (Grand Rapids, Mich.: Wm. B. Eerdmans, 1970), p. 70, and William Wiswedel, "The Handbüchlein of 1558," *Mennonite Quarterly Review,* XXIX (July, 1955), pp. 213-214.

116. Personal letter from Bill Samuel, September 16, 1976, p. 1.

117. Poem by Jessica Powers entitled "The Little Nation."

APPENDIX A

The Harassed Taxpayer's Prayer
Consider the humor of Art Buchwald who wrote the follow-
ing prayer as spoken by the harassed taxpayer:
"Heavenly Father, we beseech you in our hour of need to
look down kindly on your humble taxpaying servants who have
given all we possess to the almighty Internal Revenue Service.
Grant us that we have completed our Form 1040 correctly so
no power will find fault with it. We pray to God that we have
added lines 12, 13, 14, and 15 accurately, and that we have
subtracted line 17 from line 16 so our adjusted gross income is
computed to their divine satisfaction.

"We ask you, O Lord, to protect our exemptions and bless
our deductions as outlined in Schedule A (Form 1040) (see
Chapters 10 and 11). Have mercy on those of us who failed to
wisely estimate our payments during the year, and must now
borrow from Peter to pay Paul. Blessed are they who spent
more than they earned and contributed so much to the
economy.

"Give us strength, Lord, so that we may dwell in a lower tax
bracket forever and ever (as outlined in Publication 17, the
Revised 1972 Edition). Yea though we walk through the valley
of the shadow of bankruptcy (see tax rate schedule X, Y, Z, or
if applicable Schedule D or schedule G or maximum tax form
4726) there is no one to comfort us."

—Reprinted by permission of Art Buchwald.

APPENDIX B

The Waubee Peace Pledges
The peace pledges on page 86 grew out of a war tax retreat
held at Camp Mack in Indiana, November 4-6, 1977.

Waubee Peace Pledge I

Jesus Christ is Lord and we pledge our lives to His lordship. This is a pledge which we do make and we can make because the Lord fills His people with faith, hope, and love. This is a pledge which we make with humility, but also with conviction, aware of the risks, since under all circumstances, we must obey God rather than people.

We believe in the resurrection of Jesus Christ, knowing that it is in the resurrection that we have our life. We need follow death no more. Death is conquered. God chooses life for us.

We therefore pledge ourselves to the service of life and the renunciation of death. Jesus is the way and the truth and His way is the way of peace. We will seek to follow in that way of peace . . . and we will seek to oppose the way of war.

Specifically we make this pledge to our brothers and sisters in Christ:

1. Since we do not give our bodies for war, neither will we give our money. We will refuse payment of federal telephone taxes and federal income taxes which go for military purposes. Where our treasure is, there our hearts will be also. If our treasure is involved in making war, and if that means legal or other jeopardy for any of us, we will seek to support one another as sisters and brothers. The earth is the Lord's and the fullness thereof. Render unto God what belongs to God.

2. We further pledge ourselves to urgently communicate with brothers and sisters in our churches, urging them to join us in refusing money for war. We will also work to have annual meetings of our churches take a firm stand against payment of war taxes and to have our church agencies agree to refuse withholding of these taxes from the pay of employees. We believe that we who are the body of Christ should not serve as a military tax collection agency.

3. We further pledge ourselves to keep our hearts and lives open to the movement of God's Spirit and to follow where Jesus might lead us on the path of peace. We pray for help and guidance—that we might be instruments of God's peace.

Because we are at different points of commitment, a second

86

pledge came out of this conference. There was a common understanding by participants in the conference that Jesus is the King of Peace and that it is wrong to pay taxes for war, but for some that witness to life takes a different form.

Waubee Peace Pledge II

We, in spirit and in conscience, affirm the Waubee Peace Pledge and fully support our sisters and brothers of that covenant. At this time in our lives we feel unable to commit ourselves to nonpayment of income and phone taxes. We do commit our time, energy, and resources to searching for alternate channels of resistance, and pledge ourselves to continual seeking of God's will for us in acting definitively to oppose those taxes for payment of war.

We give thanks for the freedom given us through Christ which enables us in this search and we pray for the strength and hope to use our freedom as servants of God.

APPENDIX C

A Parable

Once, in a certain land, there were peasant villages on which napalm bombs fell; mines exploded along the paths and in the fields. Many of the villagers and their children were hurt and many killed.

When it became known that the villagers were suffering, many Christians wondered who was responsible.

A Quaker of good repute thought Congress was responsible and supported efforts to lobby the legislature to cut off funding for such bloodshed. He himself continued to give money to Congress each year on April 15 because the law said it was required.

A Catholic woman, daily communicant, thought upon the slaughter of innocent children and decided to pray each day for peace. She did not think about paying for the bombs and mines because that money was automatically taken out of her pay each week and sent to the government by her employer.

A Mennonite was troubled in conscience because he knew his taxes were paying for bombs and mines. Thinking about the future, he gave vigorous support to the World Peace Tax Fund which would provide by law that he could elect for reasons of conscience that his taxes be used only for non-military projects. He looked forward in faith to the day when this law would provide solace for his conscience.

A Baptist minister thought that the president was responsible and urged people to vote for a canditate who promised peace. Many in his congregation worked for companies making weapons; others were in the military; all were good, law-abiding citizens. The minister gave thanks to be shepherd of such a fine flock.

An elder in an Hutterian community thought upon the evils of war and recommended a relief effort to care for the families and the injured. He said, "If we knew our taxes were going only for war, of course, we would not pay them. But what can we do? Some of our taxes go for good purposes too, like schools and roads. Besides, our religious life might be disrupted if we were not faithful to the government and obedient to its laws."

Now a young man, an atheist, his eyes and heart open to suffering, made a decision to refuse to pay for war. And when the war against the villages was over and the government increased the military budget by $4 billion and continued to build nuclear weapons, he also refused to pay for this.

Which of these was neighbor to the villagers?

—By John Schuchardt. Reprinted by permission from *God and Caesar*, November, 1977.

APPENDIX D

A War Tax Protester's Letter to the Editor

I have recently received threatening letters from a terrorist group which asks that I contribute money for construction of dangerous weapons. This group makes certain claims which in the past led me to send thousands of dollars to pay for its militaristic programs. The group claimed:

1. It was concerned with peace and freedom.
2. It would provide protection for me and my family.
3. It was my duty to make these payments, and
4. I was free from personal responsibility for how this money was spent in individual cases.

Last year, for the first time, I realized that these claims were fradulent and I refused to make further payments. Although there were threats of "penalties" I am happy to report that no more serious extortion efforts have been made.

However, again this year I have been solicited to send money. In the meantime, I have ascertained that the organization which calls itself the United States of America, already has in its possession 423 B-52 and 73 FB-111 bombers with 3,800 nuclear warheads, 1,000 Minutemen missiles each with 10 megaton warheads (500 Hiroshima bombs), 54 Titan missiles with 1.5 megaton warheads or three individually targeted warheads of 160 kilotons each, 41 ballistic missiles, submarines each carrying 10 missiles with MIRVed warheads.

This group has felt the interests of peace could be served by sending 13 nuclear bombs to Israel and by selling $13 billion of the most devastating weapons to countries around the world last year. Bribery is used to promote these sales. Support is given to fascist governments rather than to democratic ones. In fact, although the entire year of 1976 was spent celebrating the American revolution, it seems that any person associated with revolution or freedom or peace today is automatically condemned. I write this letter from jail for speaking and acting for peace at the Pentagon.

May those who love their country, love their people and all people, be warned not to support this group. Its leaders talk of "first strike," "limited nuclear war," "counterforce," and "MAD"—mutual assured destruction. Can that be sanity? The cry of Wolf! Wolf! (or is it Bear! Bear!) is again being made to frighten us to pay $92 billion for 244 B-1 bombers, and to build 30 Trident submarines (the first is under construction and will carry 24 missiles, each with 17 MARV warheads. That's 408 targets, 2000 Nagasakis, three times the explosive force dropped by the United States in World War II, Korea, and Vietnam. (Remember Vietnam was 8 million tons, four times the tonnage of all of World War II). All under the command of one man.

Dear friends, I hope you may be alerted not to support this terrorist organization. They depend on your cooperation and money and usually try to collect it on April 15. They now possess a total of 30,000 nuclear bombs and each day manufacture three more at Amarillo, Texas.

Peace is not brought by bombs but by a spirit of repentance, forgiveness, and love for enemies. Let us seek a future for our children. Time is short. In eight years, 35 nations will have these weapons of terror, each one able to vaporize a city in an instant. No matter where you live, you are sitting on ground zero right now. AWAKE!

—By *John Schuchardt*, used by permission.

APPENDIX E

Unity

Refrain:
Jesus, help us live in peace.
From our blindness set us free.
Fill us with Your healing love.
Help us live in unity.

Many times we disagree
O'er what's right or wrong to do.
It's so hard to really see
From the other's point of view.
(Repeat the refrain.)

How we long for pow'r and fame.
Seeking ev'ry earthly thing.
We forget the One who came
As a servant, not a king.
(Repeat the refrain.)

—Reprinted by permission of the author, *Jerry Derstine*.

We Didn't Know
(James 1:22-25)

Chorus:
We didn't know at all,
We didn't see a thing,
You can't hold us to blame,
What could we do?
It was a terrible shame,
But we can't bear the blame,
Oh no, not us, we didn't know.

1. We didn't know said the burgomeister
   About those camps at the edge of town.
   It was Hitler and his crew that tore the German nation
      down,
   We saw the cattle cars it's true and maybe they carried a
      Jew or two,
   Woke us up as they rumbled through
   But what did you expect me to do?

2. We didn't know said the congregation,
   Singing a hymn in a church of white.
   Press was full of lies about us
   Preacher told us we were right.
   Outside agitators came and they burned some churches and
      they put the blame
   Using southern people's names to set our colored folks
      aflame.
   Maybe some of our boys got hot
   And a couple of niggers and reds got shot.
   They should've stayed where they belonged—
   The preacher would've told us if we done wrong.

3. We didn't know said the puzzled voter,
   Watching the president on TV.

Guess we gotta drop those bombs if we're gonna keep South
   Asia free.
President's such a peaceful man,
I'm sure he's got some kind of plan.
Say we're torturing prisoners of war but I can't believe that
   stuff no more,
Torturing prisoners is a communist game—
And you can bet they're doing the same.
Wish this war was over and through but what do you expect
   me to do?

—Reprinted from the Koinonia record album, "Friends."

APPENDIX G

My People, I Am Your Security

Several weeks prior to the 10th Assembly of the Mennonite
World Conference in Wichita, Kansas, in July, 1978, David H.
Janzen of Newton, Kansas, received a letter from Ladon Sheats
who is in prison for his Christian witness against the arms race.
Ladon expressed the hope that the Mennonite World
Conference would be called to confront the world-wide arma-
ments build-up.

As David fasted and prayed over this letter, the Lord spoke
the following message to him. He trembled as he wrote,
wondering what temptations or persecutions this prophecy
might bring on him. But the Lord assured him that if he
obeyed one step at a time, he could trust God with the future.
So he shared the prophecy with his congregation, the New
Creation Fellowship. The congregation confirmed it.

The statement was then presented to the Nuclear Disarmament Group of about seventy-five persons at World
Conference. They in turn arranged to have it read to the entire
assembly, urging people to respond as the Spirit of Christ
would lead them.

o   o   o

My people, proclaim to your governments and your neighbors that
you do not need armaments for your security.
   I am your security. I will give the peacemakers glory as I de-
   fended and glorified my own defenseless Son, Jesus.

My kingdom is international.
   I am pleased that my children gather all around the globe to give
   allegience to One Kingdom. My kingdom is coming in power.
   No powers, not even the powers of nuclear warfare can destroy
   my kingdom.
   My kingdom is from beyond this earth.
   The world thought it had killed Jesus, Jesus through whom I
   have overcome the world. Therefore, Be Not Afraid.

You are a gathering of my kingdom;
   My kingdom will last forever.
   Taste the first fruits now;
   Embrace the international fellowship in Christ and praise Me
   Together.

Do not fear the nuclear holocaust.
   Do not panic or take unloving short-cuts to fight the armaments
   monster.
   I go before you to do battle.

This is a spiritual battle, the battle to destroy war.
   Do not attempt to fight this battle on your own.
   Fear, guilt and anger will make you spiritual prisoners of the
   Enemy if you fight on your own authority.
   Learn to hear my voice. Learn to be at unity with those who love
   Me.
   I will lead and protect My army.
   I will co-ordinate the battle in many nations.

I want to show you where the idols of this age are hidden.
   Learn where are the missile silos, the bomb factories, the centers
   of military command, the prisons for dissenters.
   Understand that those who bow down to Fear trust in these idols
   for salvation.
   Stand beside their idols and proclaim My liberating kingdom.
   Invite them to share your life in Me. Perfect love must be your
   weapon, for perfect love casts out Fear.

If you obey My call, you will be persecuted, misunderstood, power-
less.
You will share in my suffering for the world,
But I will never abandon you. You belong to my international,
eternal kingdom.

Do not say time is running out. Do not threaten or despair.
I am the Lord of time. There is no time to seek the world's ap-
proval,
But there is time to do what I will lay before you.

By my mercy I have extended time.
I extended time for a perverse human race when I called Noah.
I lengthened the time of repentance by sending my prophets.
I have averted nuclear disaster many times for you.
Jesus offers you all time, time to repent and come to Me.
Obey my call and there will be time to do what I am laying
before you.
Now is the time.

I want you to learn who around the world has refused to bow down to
the god of fear or worship weapons of terror.
Hold hands around the world with My soldiers, My prisoners.
Pray for each other and share My strength with them.
I love those who put their trust in Me and will put joy in their
hearts.

There is time to build My kingdom.
There is time to protest armaments and to build a spiritual com-
munity for those who turn from the idols of fear.
Call them to join you in the security that flows from Father, Son
and Spirit,
My community, given for you.

My seed is planted in every one of my children;
It is waiting to break the husks of fear that it may grow toward
My Son's light.
I did not plant my spirit in Russians, or Americans, Arabs or Is-
raelis, Capitalists or Communists. . . . . that they might
destroy each other,
But that they might recognize my image in each other and come
together in praise of their creator's name.

94

My beloved children,
Share the burden of my heart,
Know my love so that you may learn to die for one another.
There is time to do this.
Trust me and I will sustain you within my kingdom forever.

—David H. Janzen

APPENDIX H

Helpful Organizations

American Friends Service Committee
160 N. 15th Street
Philadelphia, PA 19102

Brethren Service Commission
Church of the Brethren,
1451 Dundee Ave.,
Elgin, II. 60120

Catholic Worker
36 E. First Street
New York, NY 10003

Center on Law and Pacifism
300 West Apsley Street
Philadelphia, PA 19144

Central Committee for Conscientious Objectors
2016 Walnut Street
Philadelphia, PA 19103

Coalition for a New Foreign and Military Policy
120 Maryland Ave. NE
Washington, DC 20002

Conscientious Objection to Military Tax (COMIT)
2-35-18 Asahigaoka
Hino City, Tokyo 191, Japan

Fellowship of Reconciliation
Box 271
Nyack, NY 10960

Friends Committee on National Legislation
104 C. Street, N.E.
Washington, DC 20002

God and Caesar
Box 347
Newton, KS 67114

Minnesota War Tax Resistance & Alternative Fund
122 West Franklin, Room 302
Minneapolis, MN 55404

National Council for a World Peace Tax Fund
2111 Florida Ave., N.W.
Washington, DC 20008

National Interreligious Service Board
550 Washington Building
15th Street and New York Avenue, N.W.
Washington, DC 20005

Peace Pledge Union
Dick Sheppard House
6 Endsleigh Street
London, England WC1H ODX

Peacemakers
P.O. Box 627
Garberville, CA 95440

Peace Section
Mennonite Central Committee
Akron, PA 17501

Promoting Enduring Peace, Inc.
Box 103
Woodmont, CT 06460

SANE
318 Massachusetts Ave., N.E.
Washington, DC 20002

Taxation with Representation
Suite 204, 1523 L. Street, N.W.
Washington, DC 20005

Taxpayers Against War
P.O. Box 15394
San Francisco, CA 94115

War Resisters' League & War Tax Resistance
339 Lafayette Street
New York, NY 10012

The Washington Memo
Mennonite Central Committee
100 Maryland Ave., N.E.
Washington, DC 20002

Women's International League for Peace & Freedom
1213 Race Street
Philadelphia, PA 19107

Year One Newsletter
c/o Jonah House
1933 Park Avenue
Baltimore, MD 21217

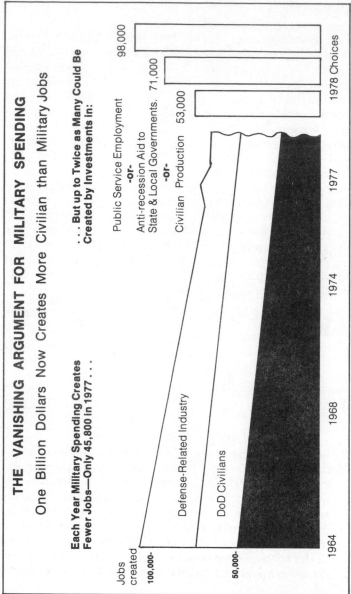

THE VANISHING ARGUMENT FOR MILITARY SPENDING

One Billion Dollars Now Creates More Civilian than Military Jobs

Each Year Military Spending Creates Fewer Jobs—Only 45,800 in 1977 . . .

. . . But up to Twice as Many Could Be Created by Investments In:

Public Service Employment   98,000

-or-

Anti-recession Aid to State & Local Governments.   71,000

-or-

Civilian Production   53,000

Jobs created

100,000-

50,000-

Defense-Related Industry

DoD Civilians

1964   1968   1974   1977   1978 Choices

Source: Center for Defense Information. Based on data from Department of Defense, Congressional Budget Office, and Bureau of Labor Statistics.

APPENDIX I

The Vanishing Argument for Military Spending

Ironically, the usual justification for labor support of the Pentagon—that military spending is good for the economy—runs contrary to a growing body of evidence. The war economy turns out to be a very poor bargain. Far from helping the economy, military spending actually contributes to unemployment, worsens inflation, and depletes the heart of the industrial economy. By diverting an excessive portion of our national wealth to the military, the nation has been spending itself into a permanent economic crisis.

Consider the following: Defense spending is one of the least efficient means of creating jobs. Almost any private or public alternative will yield more jobs per dollar than arms production. As the defense sector has become more technological, the level of overall employment has decreased. In California, for example, defense spending is currently at an all-time high, but total aerospace employment has dropped from a 1968 high of 750,000 to approximately 440,000 today.

—U.S. Senator *George McGovern* in a March, 1978, letter to constituents.

APPENDIX J

Audiovisual Resources

"Conscience and War Taxes" (Turning War Taxes into Dollars for Peace)—(20-min. 79 slide presentation with soundtrack on cassette tape.) Produced in 1978, this slide set recognizes that it is with our tax dollars that we shape the world in which we live. Because arms spending is by definition the most inflationary of all expenditures, it traces the history of the U.S. income tax, examines some of the economic consequences of military spending, and discusses a legal alternative which could provide dollars for peace instead of war. A remarkable portrayal of the responsibility of government to recognize the right of conscience on the issue of military taxes. A useful tool for educating and organizing ourselves for a more responsive tax system. Purchase price: $50 each; rental: $15 a week. Available from the National Council for a World Peace Tax Fund, 2111 Florida Ave., N. W., Washington, DC 20008. Tel. (202) 483-3751.

"Guns or Butter? Uncle Sam's Military Tapeworm" (30 min. slide set with cassette tape narration)—Exposes the growth of U.S. military spending since 1945. Through drawings, photographs and documented information, the quest for national security is portrayed as draining the resources needed for civilian programs at home and in other countries. Narrated by Paul Newman. Produced by SANE; available from either SANE, 318 Massachusetts, Ave, N.E., Washington, D.C. 20002, or from the Mennonite Central Committee, 21 S. 12th St., Akron, PA 17501.

"Hiroshima-Nagasaki, August, 1945" (16 min., b/w)—a short film edited from over three hours of footage shot by Japanese photographers just after the holocaust which killed 200,000. For 25 years the U.S. military suppressed the footage until Japanese pressure forced its release to the world. This is a very gruesome and sobering film about nuclear annihilation. Not for children below high school age. Available from Audiovisuals, Box 370, Elkhart, IN 46515.

"The Magician" (13 min., b/w)—a simple allegory about war. The children are out for play when they chance upon the "magician." He entices them into his shooting gallery where he teaches them to shoot first at targets, then at dolls, then. . . . There is only one word in this powerful story, and yet the charade of war is unmasked. Available from the American Friends Service Committee, 4211 Grand Ave., Des Moines, IA 50312, or from Audio Visual Library, Box 347, Newton, KS 67114.

"Parable" (22 min., color, sound)—a short, provocative film where no word is spoken—but you have to be spiritually deaf to miss the message. In the Gospels Jesus teaches us by using parables. . . . Today a parable might begin like this: "Once there was a great circus, and in the march of nations and peoples, a great circus parade in which some were participants, some merely spectators. A parade in which human beings seldom knew one another or cared for one another; and into this great circus of life came a man—who dared to be different." Available for purchase or rental through CINE-CATH, Catholic Missions, 371 5th St., Manistee, MI 49660.

"The Race Nobody Wins" (15 min., color slide/filmstrip with guide and cassette tape)—an inexpensive resource on the costliness of the international arms race, particularly the threat of nuclear war. Utilizes clear graphics to illustrate well-documented information. Narrated by Tony Randall. Rent or buy from SANE (A Citizen's Organization for a Sane World), 318 Massachusetts Ave., N.E. Washington, DC 20002.

"The Witness" (20 min., 16 mm. b/w film)—portrays the life of Franz Jägerstätter, a young farmer in a remote Austrian village, who discerned clearly the choice between national idolatry and the will of God. Like Jeremiah of the Old Testament, he was a man who came to realize that God and the plain moral right of the matter were no longer on the side of his country. Because of his Christian commitment he was led to "an extraordinary act of rebellion." For his conscientious objection to Hitler's militarism he was beheaded in Berlin on August 9, 1943. Film reveals in simple moving form the confrontations this passionate anti-Nazi conscientious objector had with his family, his priest, church, and state authorities. It was produced by the National Council of Catholic Men for the televised program, *The Catholic Hour*, in the mid-sixties. For a written account see Gordon Zahn's *In Solitary Witness*.

You Don't Have to Buy War, Mrs. Smith!—a documentary film produced and distributed by Another Mother for Peace, 407 North Maple Drive, Beverly Hills, CA 90210.

Donald D. Kaufman of Newton, Kansas, is currently employed as an applicator for an insulation business. Born on a farm near Marion, S. Dakota in 1933, he has served in the capacities of MCC field director, pastor, and as personnel coordinator.

He holds an MDiv degree from Associated Mennonite Biblical Seminaries, a BDiv degree from Mennonite Biblical Seminary, a BA from Bethel College, North Newton, Kansas, and an AA from Freeman Junior College, Freeman, South Dakota.

Kaufman's writing has appeared in *Sojourners, The Mennonite, Gospel Herald,* and *Pulpit Digest.* He has prepared study papers on the war tax issue as a conscientious objector to war and is author of *What Belongs to Caesar?* (Herald Press, 1969).

Donald and Eleanor (Wismer) Kaufman are members of the Bethel College Mennonite Church. They are the parents of Kendra Janean, Galen David, and Nathan Dean.

THE FOCAL PAMPHLET SERIES

1. *Integration! Who's Prejudiced?* by C. Norman Kraus, (1958).
2. *The Church and the Community,* by J. Lawrence Burkholder (1958).
3. *The Ecumenical Movement and the Faithful Church,* by John H. Yoder (1959).
4. *Biblical Revelation and Inspiration,* by Harold S. Bender (1959).
5. *As You Go,* by John H. Yoder (1961). OP
6. *The Christian Calling,* by Virgil Vogt (1961). OP
7. *The Price of Church Unity,* by Harold E. Bauman (1962).
8. *Television: Friend or Foe?* by Henry Weaver (1962).
9. *Brotherhood and Schism,* by Calvin Redekop (1963).
10. *The Call to Preach,* by Clayton Beyler (1963). OP
11. *The Church Functions with Purpose,* by Calvin Redekop (1967).
12. *Let's Talk About Extremism,* by Edgar Metzler (1968).
13. *Helping Developing Countries,* by Carl Kreider (1968). OP
14. *The Christian Stance in a Revolutionary Age,* by Donald R. Jacobs (1968).
15. *Pacifism and Biblical Nonresistance,* by J. C. Wenger (1968).
16. *Evangelicalism and Social Responsibility,* by Vernon C. Grounds (1969).
17. *World Hunger: Reality and Challenge,* by C. Franklin Bishop (1969).
18. *The Problems of Nationalism in Church-State Relationships,* by James E. Wood, Jr. (1969).
19. *Change and the Church,* by Paul N. Kraybill (1970).
20. *The City: What Is It Really Like?* by Vern Miller (1970).
21. *Ecology of the Airwaves,* by LeRoy E. Kennel (1971).
22. *Demons,* by Donald R. Jacobs (1972).
23. *Making Political Decisions,* by John R. Redekop (1972).
24. *The Spiritual Family and the Biological Family,* by Paul M. Lederach (1973).

25. *Theology: White, Black, or Christian?* by Warner Jackson (1974).
26. *Release to Those in Prison*, by William Klassen (1977).
27. *Mennonite Education: Issues, Facts, and Changes*, by Donald B. Kraybill (1978).
28. *Women in the Church*, by Dennis R. Kuhns (1978).
29. *Mennonite Identity and Literary Art*, John L. Ruth (1978).
30. *The Tax Dilemma: Praying for Peace, Paying for War*, Donald D. Kaufman (1978).

FOCAL PAMPHLETS treat timely subjects of special Christian interest and concern. They interpret and discuss problems of contemporary life as they relate to Christian truth.

Each addition to the series attempts to bring the life and thought of the Christian community into focus on a specific issue. Each pamphlet presents a valid viewpoint, but not necessarily the final word or the official position of the publisher or his constituency.

Some Focal Pamphlets grow out of intense personal study and research. Others are first prepared for presentation at special conferences or professional meetings.

The series will continue as suitable manuscripts become available.